Actually, the Comma Goes Here

Illllustrations by Rachel Joy Price

ISBN: Print 978-1-64739-922-1 | eBook 978-1-64152-650-0

R0

Actually, the Comma Goes Here

A PRACTICAL GUIDE TO PUNCTUATION

LUCY CRIPPS

PROFESSIONAL
WRITING
ACADEMY

ROCKRIDGE
PRESS

For Alison, my mother, a genuinely
wonderful human being. With love.

Contents

PUNCTUATION SNOBBERY IS DEAD.

LONG LIVE PUNCTUATION!

Meet Aristophanes, patron saint of punctuation. When Aristophanes was head librarian at Alexandria's main library, writing was a mess. Wow, were those third-century Greek philosophers, speakers, and politicians poor at getting their ideas down on parchment—even if they were great at setting up civilization.

They wrote scroll after scroll of letters written with no spaces, punctuation, or help for the reader, and Aristophanes wanted a way to help readers know how much of a pause to take. He came up with a canny method of dotting ink at the top, middle, or bottom of each line. He based the dots on the formal units of speech everyone understood at the time: comma, colon, and periods.

Yes, you do recognize them. And those dots are your first weapon in the war against punctuation snobbery, too: The original punctuation marks were genuinely about pauses or breaths. When you stick that comma in where "it feels right" . . . you would not have been far wrong if you were ancient Greek. Go ahead and share that with anyone who says your comma, colon, or period is out of place.

My love affair with punctuation started about a decade ago, so I remember all too well the gut-wrench of being out of your depth, up against someone who thinks they know best. I had just started lecturing at Salzburg University in Austria, and I had been ~~landed with~~ awarded the advanced writing course.

Being a native speaker, I knew intuitively where the marks went, but explaining why was a whole different story. The undergraduates were so far ahead of me in their knowledge of English grammar. To catch up, I started a painful journey of very late nights, of learning the next day's lesson inside out, of exploring every question from the last lesson, and of guessing their next round of quizzing. I read every book I could get my hands on and confused myself until I understood.

As with anything you put so much time and emotion into, I fell for punctuation. It made sense to me. It was—is—logical. Now when I see punctuation wobbles, they are a source of comedy rather than confusion. Recently, I saw this delight on the back of a truck: "Fast dog food delivery service." Is that a spritely dog delivering food (fast-dog food-delivery service) or dog food delivered to your door at speed (a fast dog-food delivery service)?

What about the joy of a missed serial comma? For instance: "I'd like to thank my parents, the queen and God"—that is one well-connected individual—rather than "I'd like to thank my parents, the queen, and God," which is far more likely.

I promise you punctuation is not a secret code; it is a way for everyone to understand each other—it is the very opposite of snobbery. Just as Aristophanes planned it.

Forget blustering punctuation snobs. The rules of punctuation are easy enough for elementary school children to understand—and they do. And with this book, you will learn those rules and pick up perfect comebacks to put those punctuation pedants right back in their place.

It's a Matter of Style

So why all the punctuation pedants, who almost always have different ideas of what constitutes proper punctuation? Blame style guides.

US punctuation rules are clear, but differences in use appear depending on your writing purpose and its prescribed style. Journalists follow the *Associated Press* (AP) style guide tweaked to a house style, often completely different to other publications' styles.

Academics writing journal papers follow *Modern Language Association* (MLA) or, for research, maybe *Turabian*. Writers working with engineering, social sciences, and business use *American Psychological Association* (APA); lawyers turn to *The Blue Book*; and—as with this book—fiction and nonfiction authors rely on the *Chicago Manual of Style* (CMS), often with an additional, possibly contradictory, house style sheet.

So when someone comes at you with their "you've missed a comma, here," or "you've missed the hyphen in nonfiction," you can respond with divine calm that you are using a house style.

For combating snobbery, punctuation styles give us excellent breathing space.

Belly Laugh of Irony

The CMS rule for colons is not to capitalize after a colon "unless it is a proper noun or more than two sentences following the colon." But the house style for this book uses a cap after the colon "if it introduces a complete sentence." So I cap after the colon. House style wins.

This book focuses on the *Chicago Manual of Style*, but there is a cheat sheet at the back to help you navigate the main styles' differences.

CHAPTER ONE
THE PERIOD

Here he comes, the granddaddy of punctuation, the period. What he says goes—no messing around.

He has ruled the roost since the beginning of punctuation time, when he helped Aristophanes help the fathers of civilization. The period is stern, opinionated, and unswayable. He holds entire sentences and sentence fragments to rights and clears space for the rest of punctuation to do its thing.

There Is Something You Need to Know

Before we get to grips with the period, we need to check in with what sentences and sentence fragments are.

Sentences

There are two types of sentence that need a period: declarative and imperative. Both express a complete statement and can be understood without context.

Declarative Sentence

A declarative sentence must have at least *one subject* and **one verb**.

> *This* **is** a sentence.

> *More than one word* **can make up** a subject.

Notice all the declarative sentences have a *subject* and a **verb** (or **phrasal verb**).

Imperative Sentence

And notice, too, that the last sentence does not follow the same pattern but still makes sense. It is an imperative sentence, starting with the verb "notice." The "you" is implied.

> **Look** carefully and *you'll* **understand.**

> **Sit. Eat.**

Generally starting with a verb in its root form (not ending with an "-ed" or "-ing"), the imperative sentence is a command and ends in a period (not, as many believe, an exclamation point).

Sentence Fragments

Fabulous little things, sentence fragments really get the punctuation snobs in a lather. Fragments offer the most powerful writing we have. Single words. Rogue rule breakers. They make more of a point than any long-winded sentence.

They start with nouns, adjectives, adverbs—whatever you want—and, possibly best of all, they can start with "and," "but," or "so," too. And to hell with the rules.

"You're right," you can say to your resident pedant, "sentences can't start with 'and,' 'but,' or 'so,' but sentence fragments can. Glorious." And feel free to turn on your heel and flounce.

Use to End Sentences and Sentence Fragments

The period ends most sentences and sentence fragments. The rest of the time, exclamation points (sometimes too often) and question marks stand in.

So you start your sentence with a capital letter, throw in your subject, your verb, maybe a direct and indirect object, pepper the sentence with a couple of phrases and tell the readers you have finished with a period. Simple as that. And that. Leave a space (or two if you are writing science), grab a capital letter, and start the next sentence.

If you are fond of sentence fragments, remember that they still need to make sense contextually. Or they'll never eat their dinner.

See the point? Fragments are grammatically and rhetorically joyful, but they only work if the sentences around them are strong enough to carry them.

PUNCTUATION HISTORY
The Period

One of the first punctuation marks created by Aristophanes and the only one that still looks the same, the period has been around for more than two thousand years. Back in the day, it sat at the top of the last letter, but from around the ninth century, it started settling at the bottom. At that time, it still marked how long a speaker should pause—of all the marks, its pause was the longest.

As grammar moved from being a spoken function to a written one, a whole new set of rules built up around the period. There is a little clue to these changes in the British use of the end-of-sentence dot. They call it a full stop. How very final.

Originally, the period referred to a period of time (as it still does in one definition of the word) or an entire thought, and the full stop signaled the end of that, so technically it was a full stop at the end of the period . . . like the curtain dropping (full stop) on the end of the show (period).

But as time marched on, the period came to mean the mark at the end of the US sentence, and the British had a "full stop." Same thing. Same rules. Different word.

Now in the world of dot-coms and www., maybe the period and full stop will once again merge, and we will all go back to the "dot" Aristophanes started out with. Food for thought.

Be careful, though. Overusing periods can mess things up. Too many, and writing gets a staccato feel to it. You lose flow. Thankfully we have a whole nest of other punctuation marks we can use to avoid such drama.

Use for Abbreviations, Acronyms, and Initials

The period. How can something so small cause such arguments? Abbreviations, acronyms, and initials help us. But since the punctuation pedants got their hands on them, confusion is rife. Again, though, disagreement between punctuation snobs helps the rest of us.

Initials

When a pedant says "U.S.A." absolutely must have periods after each letter, come out, all guns blazing. None of the style guides has this rule. In some instances news outlets use a period between two-word initials of proper nouns (U.S., U.K., U.N.), but between three-word initials, never.

Just enjoy that for a moment.

News publications use periods without spaces between initials for names (A.A. Milne, J.K. Rowling, George R.R. Martin), but all other styles use a period and a space between initials (A. A. Milne, J. K. Rowling, George R. R. Martin).

Abbreviations

If an abbreviation ends in a capital letter—CD, DVD, GPA, IP—it has no period. If it ends in a lowercase letter, it takes a period: Dr., Mr., Mrs., Jr.

But, if you have a pedant on your back, and that period slipped, here is your talking point: "Oh, of course! Did you know the Brits do not use a period after lowercase abbreviations (except "etc.")? I guess if I'd missed the period in Mr, Mrs, and Dr over there, I'd be fine."

Something no one agrees on, style wise, are periods in abbreviations of states, provinces, and the District of Columbia. This plays in our favor because if they cannot decide, why should we?

Acronyms

None of the style guides wants a period between acronyms, like social-media favorites FOMO, YOLO, DM, IMO, and the more serious AIDS, NAFTA, and NASA. So YDY.

Periods and Other Punctuation

It is not uncommon to have direct quotes, parentheses, and question marks or exclamation points hanging around at the end of the sentence, too. So how do we fit them around the period? For the most part, if there is another period, maybe from an ellipsis, abbreviation, or initial, you drop the period.

> I love chatting about grammar, etymology, punctuation, etc.

> You have to love *Iron Man*, played by Robert Downey Jr.

With quotation marks and a complete sentence within parentheses, keep the period inside.

> He said, "Now I get it." (I wish it were always this easy.)

One Space or Two After the Period?

For centuries, typesetters have swung between single and double spacing after the period, depending on the machinery available: manual printing presses, typewriters, and now HTML. This particular punctuation peccadillo is not new.

Most style guides now call for single spacing; only the science-focused APA doubles up. But there are individuals who vocally stand by the double spacing they learned 40-plus years ago. Technically, though, there is no reason for the pedants to dictate—unless they are paying you. If you prefer two, go for it—spread out. But, and this is vital, be consistent. And never, ever go beyond a double space.

There is one exception. Of course there is. If there is information outside the end-of-sentence parentheses, the period goes outside the parentheses.

She finally understood (but it hadn't been easy).

And that is all you need to know about the period. **Period.**

CHAPTER TWO
THE COMMA

With Southern charm, commas elegantly guide the reader through beautifully crafted sentences, tweaking a place setting here, adjusting the silverware there.

Like the southern belle, the comma follows strict rules and has impeccable skills that take her artistry to another level, with a twinkling "yes, ma'am" that beguiles and belies her strength. The comma guides, acknowledges, and responds with utter grace, sweet tea in hand.

When used properly, commas keep writing flowing while helping each sentence to make sense, stopping clauses and phrases from crashing into each other or changing the sentence's meaning.

There is little doubt, though, that commas can traumatize. They have rules and uses galore—more than any other punctuation marks but while some commas are absolute musts, others are down to us and our personal style.

The modern comma joined the ranks of punctuation back in the 1400s. That is a long time for rules to grow, blossom, and mature, and for exceptions to pile on exceptions. But around 1997, R. L. Trask, longtime American-British grammarian and punctuation guru, whittled the centuries of comma rules to four types: the listing comma, the joining comma, the gapping comma, and bracketing commas. And he detailed them in *The Penguin Guide to Punctuation*, which can really help when a punctuation snob is lurking.

Still. Getting those top-level comma rules sorted does not have to be a struggle. Let us pull on our confidence again where commas are concerned.

Use for Items in a Series

OK, we should start with a) the simplest comma use, and b) the most contentious: commas that separate items in a series of three or more elements.

> My favorite things are grammar, punctuation, and books about grammar and punctuation.

Easy, right? US style guides say put a comma between each item, including before the "and." So that is what we do. Now we can move on. Except we cannot. Because newspapers, the most common way the country sees words and sentences written out, do not use a serial comma before that "and." They prefer this:

> My favorite things are grammar, punctuation and books about grammar and punctuation.

But to add to the arguments, the **Associated Press** tells us to use a comma if leaving one out would make the sentence ambiguous or confusing. This is the **Harvard comma** or **Oxford comma** you hear people barking about. But what might "confusing" look like? Earlier, we had this:

> "I'd like to thank my parents, the queen and God."

and

> "I'd like to thank my parents, the queen, and God."

That serial comma makes it clear the parents are not the queen and God, but they are two of the three entities the person wants to thank: 1. the parents, 2. the queen, 3. God.

So why not just use the comma every time before the "and" in a series? Good question! Just add the comma plus "and" and all will be well, unless you are an AP journalist and an editor is on your back telling you to drop it.

Use to Connect Independent Clauses

Before we sling on our backpacks and venture further into the comma world, we should check in with clauses.

An independent clause is, essentially, a sentence, so it must have a subject and a verb—and make sense on its own. We can load our sentences with independent clauses as long as each one joins the next with a comma and a coordinating conjunction.

There are seven coordinating conjunctions, often known as the **FANBOYS: f**or, **a**nd, **n**or, **b**ut, **o**r, **y**et, **s**o.

> This is an independent clause, **and** this is an independent clause.
>
> Each independent clause makes sense on its own, **but** it links very closely in theme to the other independent clause.

In the news business, **Associated Press** says that if the two independent clauses are short, we can leave the comma out.

> I cook and I eat.

AP does love leaving out a comma, doesn't it?

Careful Now!

Some things to be wary of are compound subjects and compound verbs in what, at first glance, might seem like an independent clause:

> They **lit** the grill but **had forgotten** to bring the steaks.

(compound verbs—two or more verbs in one clause)

PUNCTUATION HISTORY
The Comma

Other than the period, the comma is the most common punctuation mark in English. Back in the late 1400s, Venetian printer Aldus Manutius gave the world the modern comma when writing was still what Aristotle called "the representation of speech." It was a time when the early-Renaissance kids were using a slash to show a pause in speech. But slashes used way too much of Manutius's ink and too much space in the groundbreaking portable books he was planning on changing the world with.

He took it upon himself to chop the slash in half, give it a gentle curve, and lower it to the line—and the first comma was born. As one of only a few pioneering printers committed to taking reading and books to the masses, he pretty much had the monopoly on punctuation invention, so his comma was the first most people who could read saw. And if it ain't broke, don't fix it, right? So the comma we have today is exactly as it was back in Renaissance Venice. Nothing about how it looks has changed.

But how we use it has changed. A lot. It started life marking pauses in speech, but over the centuries it has gathered a stunning range of uses. Arlene Miller's *To Comma or NOT To Comma* lists a staggering 30 uses, some with subsections and exceptions, and one simply named "Gray Areas."

A really old boat and a *funny-looking pirate* **appeared** on the river.

(compound subject—two or more subjects in the same clause)

These coordinating conjunctions (FANBOYS) do not have commas before them because they are not joining two or more independent clauses.

Use to Separate Dependent Clauses

Dependent clauses are as needy as they sound: They are not allowed out without an independent clause. They need their own subject and verb, but they also have a subordinate conjunction or relative pronoun to mark them as dependent.

Common subordinating conjunctions: after, when, since, if, because, although, despite, etc.

Common relative pronouns: that, which, who, whom, whichever, etc.

As for the comma, if the dependent clause comes before the independent clause, we add a comma after the dependent clause and before the independent clause. Like this:

> **If the dependent clause comes before the independent clause,**
> we add a comma after the dependent clause.

When the dependent clause follows an independent clause, most style guides do not use a comma. Like this:

> Most style guides do not use a comma **when a dependent clause follows an independent clause.**

The fun with the dependent clause is we can shunt it around to help the whole sentence fit the sentences around it. Look at the difference between

> I heard it was going to rain this afternoon. We'll eat our picnic in the backyard because it hasn't.

and

> I heard it was going to rain this afternoon. Because it hasn't, we'll eat our picnic in the backyard.

In the second sentence, shifting that dependent clause into the first position means we have two sentences that flow logically. And who does not love logic?

What about the comma before "because"? Good question. We only need a comma before "because" if the sentence could be misunderstood without it. Using a blanket comma plus "because" is wrong.

Use for Nonessential Clauses

Nonessential clauses are dependent clauses that are interesting but not "essential" to the meaning of the sentence. Hence the name. If the nonessential clause disappeared, nothing would be lost. See here:

Essential:

> The email **that** I got last week explained the situation perfectly.

Nonessential:

> The email, **which** I got last week, explained the situation perfectly.

Without commas, the first example has essential information specifically about a week-old email that explained a situation. There may have been other emails since that were pretty bad at explaining the situation.

The second example has nonessential information. By using the commas and "which," we show we do not care about when the email arrived, simply that it explained everything. It is irrelevant that the email arrived last week. Nice. But not essential.

When you get the hang of "that" and "which," things are pretty easy for "who," "where," "whom," and so on, too. See how they play out:

"Who"

Essential:

> My sister who really annoys me just dropped by for lunch without calling.

(One annoying sister.)

Nonessential:

> My sister, who really annoys me, just dropped by for lunch without calling.

(More sisters, one of them is annoying.)

"Where"

Essential:

> The store where I get the milk is across the street.

(Maybe the best store of many for milk.)

Nonessential:

> The store, where I get the milk, is across the street.

(One store.)

"Whom"

Essential:

> The guy whom I sit next to in class is very smart.

(The guy *I* sit next to is very smart—there might be other smart guys in class, too.)

Nonessential:

> The guy, whom I sit next to in class, is very smart.

(One guy is too smart.)

Use for Introductory Words or Phrases

Think of children's writing—so many sentences starting with the subject, either "I" or "The something-or-other." Cute for kids. Not so much for adults. Adding introductory words and phrases give sentences a bit of life.

Before we get into commas, a word about phrases. Whilst a clause needs a subject and verb to be seen in public, a phrase does not. A phrase is a single word or cluster of words and needs neither a subject nor a verb.

Introductory words and phrases—let us call them "the junk at the front"—are anything before the subject (or imperative verb if that is more your thing) at the beginning of a sentence. They add a little va-va-voom and oo-la-la to sentences, and they come in several shapes and sizes.

> **Patting herself on the back,** she added an amazing introductory phrase.
>
> **Delighted by her clean house,** she poured a glass of wine and settled in for the evening.
>
> **Head of English,** Mr. Wobblesworthy was a very gifted linguist.
>
> **On Sunday,** we will dress up nicely and go for dinner somewhere special.

To keep punctuation snobs off your back, assume you need a comma after all introductory words and phrases.

There is one exception. Single- or two-word introductory elements are fine without a comma—see how this comma interrupts the mojo of the sentence:

Last week we ate a huge chocolate cake.

Last week, we ate a huge chocolate cake.

In short introductory elements, adding a comma is about style and flow, and every bit your call.

Use for Appositive Phrases

Appositives are little nuggets of lovely. "But they sound so swish, so complicated," you say. But appositives are, quite simply, nouns or noun phrases that sit by another noun or noun phrase to add information or description. We can spot an appositive because it starts with "a," "the," or a common or proper noun.

An appositive, **a noun or noun phrase,** adds a nugget of lovely to a sentence.

If the appositive is mid-sentence, say between the subject and the verb, we need to bracket the noun phrase with commas. The front-of-the-sentence appositive follows "junk in the front" rules and takes a comma after it.

> **A big buffoon in most things,** my best friend is excellent at spotting appositives.

The end-of-sentence appositive needs a comma before it. Like this:

> Smashing her deadline, she poured herself a tea, **a glorious hug in a mug.**

Adding commas around appositives is important for avoiding awkward situations. Look here:

> My husband, **Steve,** unloads a dishwasher like a legend.

"Steve" is appositive, adding information—his name—to "my husband." It is clear there is only one husband: Steve. Remove the comma, though, and all hell breaks loose:

> My husband **Steve** unloads a dishwasher like a legend.

Here, no-comma "Steve" is one of many. Maybe husband Steve is dishwasher king, and husband Bob is better at yard work. Husband John cooks a mean steak.

Prepare to impress your resident punctuation pedant with an, "Oh, look, you need a comma after/before/around that appositive." Your very own mic-drop moment.

Use for Descriptors

Like appositives, descriptors add—surprise!—description. But instead of nouns, descriptors are adjectives, adverbs, and prepositional phrases. Elementary school taught us that adjectives describe nouns, adverbs help verbs, and prepositional phrases put the noun or verb in a particular place, time, reason, or manner.

Adjective:

> The child, **happy and excited,** ran into the sea.

Adverb:

> The guilty teenager, **noisily and poorly,** hid the console controller.

Prepositional phrase:

> The mother, **with astonishing patience,** taught her son to cook dinner.

Descriptors are fun to play with. We can shift them before or after the word or phrase they describe—but do not move them too far away. See how shunting adjectives around changes the rhythm of these sentences and drops the last one into chaos.

> **Happy and excited,** the child ran into the sea.
>
> The child ran, **happy and excited,** into the sea.
>
> The child ran into the sea, **happy and excited.**
>
> The child ran into the, **happy and excited,** sea.

Clearly, that last one really does not work. Why? Because the descriptor is too far from its noun.

Right. To commas. Commas keep descriptors in check, caged in. But we do have an element of freedom, especially with adverb and prepositional phrase descriptors—we can leave commas out if we feel they play with the rhythm of the sentence too much.

We naturally emphasize the word before the comma and slightly emphasize the words inside the commas, so try reading out loud what you have written to see if keeping or leaving out a comma works better.

Use for Direct Address

An easier way of saying "direct address" is "talking to someone, using their name." Breaking the mysteries of punctuation down, bit by bit, here.

When you are talking to someone and using their name or a word they know means them ("darling," "sweetie," "oi," "sir"), that word-name needs commas. This is not challenging, but so many people start emails with "Hi Steve" rather than "Hi, Steve," or the word-name of the person they are addressing. Just remember to use a comma here.

> **Mom,** how do I boil the potatoes?
>
> **Dude,** where's my car?
>
> Have a wonderful evening, **darling.**
>
> **You, sweetie,** make the best fried green tomatoes.
>
> Hey, **sir.**
>
> Good afternoon, **everyone.**
>
> Excuse me, **miss.**

Get the gist? These commas are so easy to spot and correct, so the moment your resident pedant has pushed you to the limits, you can probably dip into an old email and feel smug when you see he or she has missed the comma. You're welcome.

Word of warning: Dear John, Dear Sirs, and Dear Mrs. Cripps, etc., do NOT need a comma after "dear." The "dear" is an adjective, describing how you feel about that person (OK, they might not be all that dear, but we have to play nice).

And just an FYI: Responses, like "yes," "no," "ah, gee," "well," and whatnot, also need a comma after them. It can get a bit comma cramped in there:

> **"Hi, Jenny, uh,** how are we fixed for this evening?"

> **"Well, you know, Mike,** I'm pretty sure everything will be fine."

> **"Great, Jenny,** see you there!"

Use for Quotations

When we think "quotations," we nod sagely and mutter about quotation marks. But when we have a wonderfully put-together utterance that says perfectly what we want to say, quotation marks are not strong enough on their own.

Commas clear the way for an epic quotation and, after it, give the reader a moment to take in its fantasticness before continuing with the sentence or paragraph.

Thankfully, there is no mystery with commas and quotation marks—we just have to remember to use them. But where?

Here:

> Introduce the quotation, **(comma)** "Astounding quotation, **(comma inside the quotation marks)**" and finish with an attribution **(who said it)** or a little comment about the astounding quotation.

HOW TO BEAT THE SNOBS
The Serial Comma

With so many uses and styles, commas are a hotbed of contention for punctuation pedants. Possibly the biggest argument surrounds the serial comma—we are talking finger-pointing, furrowed brows, and even a little frothing at the mouth. This is serious stuff.

As we now know, the serial comma, aka **Harvard comma**, aka **Oxford comma**, is the comma before the "and" in a list of three or more items. Essentially, some people use it, and others do not. And why people get so hot under the collar about it is possibly because it is one of the simplest rules out there. It is easy to be absolutely confident about (unlike, say, nonessential clauses). It is easy to choose a side and stick to it.

For a sniff of the emotion attached to the serial comma, pop back to 2011 when the punctuation world went into fabulous meltdown. A rumor emerged that Oxford University Press had stopped using the Oxford comma, and social media lost its sweet mind. Just search "serial comma" on Twitter—you will be glad you did.

What did Oxford University Press have to say about it? They blew the whole kerfuffle out of the water, standing by its house style of using the Oxford comma. Now and forever. Amen.

And the style guides? *For* the serial comma: CMS and most US publishers. *Against it:* Associated Press and most US media outlets, unless leaving it out causes confusion.

For example:

> **In his extreme wisdom, author Oscar Wilde mused, "I am not young enough to know everything," a sentiment I could not agree with more, now that I have preteens in the house.**

Simple as that.

Quick note: If your quotation takes up more than two lines or is longer than two sentences, you introduce it with a colon, not a comma. (See the chapter on colons.)

Double-quick note: We should only use truly special quotations. They should say perfectly what we want to say. They should not be mundane and throwaway—use quotations only if we cannot paraphrase the idea in a better way.

There is a whole other chapter about quotation marks, so head thataway if you want to know more.

CHAPTER THREE
THE APOSTROPHE

The apostrophe has a rough time of it, abused left, right, and center by people just scattering it around to make plurals, incorrect possession, and all sorts of nonsense. I am not one to align with the pedants, but we have to feel for the apostrophe.

With just three fundamental uses, it is literally one of the easiest punctuation marks to use, but the apostrophe leaves the majority of people in a quandary. A bit like a jealous girlfriend, the apostrophe is possessive and whiny about feeling left out. But since the 16th century, when Shakespeare et al. simply slipped the apostrophe comfortably into a space to indicate a missing letter in their poetic wanderings, it has thrown its weight around, confusing all and sundry.

Look back through history, and there seems never to have been a time when the apostrophe's rules were understood properly even by those in the know. We need to change that. Now.

We should get two things cleared up, right off the bat.

1. Apostrophes DO NOT create plurals.

Something you will quickly spot is the lack of rule for using an apostrophe to show plurals. **BECAUSE IT DOES NOT EXIST**. If there is more than one carrot, we write about the "carrots." No apostrophe.

2. Apostrophes are NOT allowed near possessive pronouns.
(They are possessive enough already.) Another easy way to avoid embarrassment is never to allow apostrophes anywhere near a pronoun:

> **mine**
>
> **yours** (not your's)
>
> **ours** (not our's)
>
> **hers** (not her's)
>
> **theirs** (not their's)
>
> **whose** ("who's" means "who is"—a different thing altogether)

Use for Contractions—or Missing Letters

Not much is as simple as contraction apostrophes. All we do is switch out a letter for an apostrophe.

This is what the apostrophe was created for, its birthright: to stand in for letters dropped to keep the rhythm of the sentence. Shakespeare, for one, loved a contraction apostrophe, as we see in this barrel of laughs from *Richard II* [III, 3]:

> If not, I'll use the advantage of my power **(I will)**
>
> And lay the summer's dust with showers of blood **(This is a possessive apostrophe. Move on.)**
>
> Rain'd from the wounds of slaughter'd Englishmen **(rained, slaughtered)**

Fast-forward, and we still love to remove a letter and stick in an apostrophe. It makes reading a whole lot easier.

> It is so simple. **(It's so simple.)**
>
> She would have said yes if I had asked nicely. **(She'd've said yes if I'd asked nicely.)**

Using apostrophes for number contractions is also a thing—but not, **NOT**, for creating plurals.

A contraction might mean replacing "19" of 1990s with an apostrophe, making it '90s. Simple. Or so you would think.

But some joker decided this number apostrophe is actually the possessive apostrophe before the "s," thus: 90's. And it stuck. This apostrophe is so widespread now that even pedants wander off the accuracy tracks.

"The music of the 90's is by far the best," says the punctuation pedant.

"Oh, no, the '90s had the best music," you can respond.

. . . quietly smug as you adjust your apostrophe halo.

Use for Singular Possession

If we want to show that one thing belongs to something else, we could either create a sentence using "of," or just add an apostrophe+s.

The grandma of my friend **(my friend's grandma)**

This works in the vast majority of cases.

The cat's tail

The dog's mouth

The mother's favorite terrarium

The family's best sofa

It is the same if the nouns end in "s" and adding it creates a "z" sound:

The boss's visit

The hostess's last chance

OK, hold the mini saga a moment. If the word that follows the "s" starts with an "s," those AP news hounds (and some book publishers) would drop the "s" after the apostrophe. Like this:

The boss' scowl

The hostess' squeal

And the newsroom would also just go with an apostrophe after an "s" in a name.

Jess' quiet terror

Mr. Jones' silent fury.

While the rest of us would hide behind the sofa, following

Jess's quiet terror and

Mr. Jones's silent fury

. . . and wonder what on earth would happen next.

A quick note: "It's" is NOT in the possessive family. "It's" is a contraction for "it is." To make sure we get this right, every time, all we have to do is read "it's" as "it is."

Use for Plural Possession

Plural apostrophes are terrors because plurals come with their own "s" fitted as standard:

witches

Munchkins

flying monkeys

HISTORY LESSON
The Apostrophe

An old Latin teacher of mine, Mrs. D, would talk over our yawns and snores to impart surprisingly useful nuggets of information about English grammar, which she was passionate about.

We would hear "Blah, blah, blah, something about Latin," then one day, something she said got through. "But, listen, puellae, if you are going to take letters out of your writing, the least you can do is replace those letters with an apostrophe. If you sneaked out at night, which, puellae, I'm sure you'd never do, you would put pillows in your bed to make it look like you're still there, wouldn't you?

"Think of apostrophes as the valiant pillows standing in your stead, prepared to take the fall when you're not there.

"Missing letters might be at the end of sentences, and they might be whole words. Think: 'Mrs. D's book' is just another way of saying 'The book of Mrs. D,' and 'the girls' future,' just another way of saying 'the future of the girls.' Remember the pillows, puellae, remember the pillows."

All familiar, commonplace plurals you might find around the house. And not an apostrophe to be seen. That is because they are currently just plurals and no wicked witch has tried to take possession of them. Yet.

In securing possession of them, who knew Dorothy could have left the ruby slippers at home and just thrown some apostrophes around?

Her Munchkins' chores

The ruby slippers' new owner was soon on her way to Oz

The flying monkeys' screams are pretty terrifying

Now that that headache is over, we need to visit plurals not ending in "s," like:

women

men

children

For these, we add an apostrophe+s:

the women's screwdrivers and the men's cakes were getting in the children's way

They work exactly like singular possessives.

But here's a plural quandry. What should happen here?

Dot your is and cross your ts

All style guides agree that for lowercase plural letters, we use an apostrophe:

Dot your i's and cross your t's

But get into capitalized plurals, and the gloves come off. CMS says nay to apostrophes in capitalized plural letters, but the AP news guys want to see them:

I like the Ms, Ts, and, most especially, the Zs (CMS)

versus

I like the M's, T's, and, most especially, the Z's **(AP)**

But Associated Press nixes apostrophes with capital-letter clusters: ERs, TVs, VRs. MLA and APA just ignore the problem but do express a dislike for apostrophes in TVs, EQs, and VIPs.

Use for Shared Possession

For that chat about two people who share or have independent possession of a thing, there is a super-useful apostrophe.

Not many people would say:

First, we'll swing by the house of Lucy and Steve

We would say

First, we'll swing by Lucy and Steve's house

See that "'s" after "Steve"—and notice "Lucy" does not have one? That tells us they live at the same house. If we use an apostrophe after each person, we know we would be popping by two separate houses:

Sam's and Jo's house

Although "house" is not plural, because both names have "'s," we know we are going to Sam's house first, then Jo's. And while there, maybe we get to know

Sam's and Jo's friends

Because they have different sets of friends. It's going to be a social drive-about. Now, if we are going to a family's house, we follow the same rules as singular and plural possessives. Nothing changes just because it is a name. Let us visit the French family. They are a really nice bunch.

Singular:

Mrs. French's house

Plural:

Mr. and Mrs. French are **the Frenches** (not the French's)

Plural possessive:

Party at the Frenches' house!

HOW TO BEAT THE SNOBS
Apostrophe Woes

Simply by existing, the apostrophe has tamed large national associations and international bodies that are unsure of how to accommodate it. The cannier associations across the globe have got it sorted by shifting words around:

Jewelers of America (US)

National Association of Jewellers (GB)

(Note the additional "l" in the British form of "Jewelers.")

But we all know why these are the names they chose—because National Jewelers' Association has that confounded apostrophe . . . or does it?! And therein lies the problem.

For most of us, whether large groups, gatherings, and associations need apostrophes is fairly irrelevant, and a quick look at the material produced by the association will answer the question. If the people in the association want an apostrophe, all power to them. Use it.

In our day-to-day writing, we are far more likely to come up against the "possessive apostrophe versus adjective" problem.

> **Farmers' market** or farmers market
>
> **Kids' menu** or kids menu
>
> **Teachers' strike** or teachers strike

With the apostrophe, we are saying that the market, menu, or strike belongs to the farmers, kids, or teachers, which is fine.

Here is a thought: What if we look at "farmers," "kids," or "teachers" as adjectives—words to describe the words that follow them? Then we do not use the apostrophe. And this is a battle still underway between the heavyweight style guides, which gives us a very handy fence to sit on.

> Associated Press: **no apostrophe (farmers market)**
>
> Chicago Manual of Style: **apostrophe (farmers' market)**

Take your pick.

Oh, and by the way, it is **never:**

> **Farmer's market** (one single, lonely farmer)
>
> **Kid's menu** (a whole menu for one child)
>
> **Teacher's strike** (not exactly people power)

And the same with names ending in "s."

Singular:

Lucy Cripps's house

Plural:

Lucy and Steve Cripps are the Crippses (add that –es to show we are plural)

Plural possessive:

After party at the Crippses' house

It is a bring-your-own-bottle party, by the way. Please RSVP. (Punctuation pedants need not apply.)

CHAPTER FOUR
THE QUESTION MARK

One of the depressingly named *terminal* punctuation marks, the question mark also goes by "interrogation point" and has pretty much one job: to ask a question.

Does the question mark mark a question? That it does. Press pass in hat, the question mark is always on the hunt for the next big story, looking for the why, what, where, who, and when. He crafts wily questions to get to the bottom of the world's biggest mysteries and problems.

But in an exciting turn of events, in 2011, the sleuthing question mark was itself sleuthed by a Cambridge professor called Chip.

Manuscript specialist Chip—Dr. Coakley—discovered that the question mark is the great-great-great (and some) grandson of the **zawga elaya**, a vertical double question dot used in ancient Syriac.

That puts it first in line to the question-mark throne, making it older than the Greek interrogation point (the fabulously named **eroteme**), and older than the shortened version of Latin's **quæstio**, "Qo," which many people peg as the origin of the question mark.

Starring Question Mark

Question mark's most entertaining role is a collab with the exclamation point. Together, they create the most exciting punctuation point, ever: **the interrobang** or **interabang**. The interrobang (officially ‽ but often just ?!, !?, or ?!?) adds—with exceptional panache—excitement or disbelief to proceedings.

> **What on Earth are you wearing?!**

> **You think the comma is the best punctuation mark?!**

It is hard to not love an interrobang and, in turn, the question mark.

Use Question Marks to Ask Questions

We ask a question by adding a question mark (?) to the end of our phrase, clause, or sentence fragment:

Do you understand?

Got it?

Really?

Questions can appear in all sorts of places in a sentence. If the question is at the beginning of a sentence, we put the question mark at the end of the question—not the end of the sentence. See what happens if we put the question mark at the end of the sentence:

Where does the question mark go is the question?

Where does the question mark go? is the question.

The meaning shifts from being about the question mark to being about the question asked.

Obviously, if the end of the question is also the end of the sentence, we use a question mark and no period. The question mark always kicks the period and the comma out of play.

We might have a whole flurry of questions we need to fire out but do not have time or inclination to make each one a sentence on its own. In this case, we can either have a question mark at the end of each question and start the next question with a lower-case letter, or we can bundle them all into a sentence ending in a question mark:

The party is tomorrow: Who's hanging the bunting? who'll make the cake? who'll jump out of the cake?

The party is tomorrow: Who's hanging the bunting, who'll make the cake, who'll jump out of the cake?

How to Use a Question Mark in a Non-Question

Questions do not always want or need an answer. They are like that. Sometimes they are loaded with opinion or judgment. On the face of it, they are merely phrases:

> You're wearing pants.

> I've eaten bugs.

Without the question mark, it looks a whole lot like a statement. But stick a question mark on the end, and look what happens. Boom—you have a question loaded with opinion:

> **You're wearing pants?**

> **I've eaten bugs?**

Another not-really-a-question is the question tag. It can do almost the same as the judgey question-statement.

> You're not wearing pants, are you?

> You're wearing pants, are you?

But question tags are not always sneery. They are incredibly useful for continuing conversation or showing interest. "Tell me more," says the question tag.

> You like eating insects, do you?

> There's a reason I shouldn't be wearing pants, isn't there?

You get this, right?

Question tags at the end of the sentence always need a question mark, but if the question tag appears mid-sentence, we would leave it out.

You know how to use a question tag, don't you?

You know, don't you, how to use a question tag.

And finally, if we are not entirely sure about something—say a birth date, death date, or maybe a large number—we add the question mark in parentheses:

There were so many people **(100,000+?)** at the gig, they couldn't count them all.

Early humans started playing with fire around 1.42 million years **(?)** ago.

And on that bombshell, we should move on.

When Not to Use a Question Mark

When we report questions, we do not use question marks because the sentence, as a whole, is a statement rather than a question.

She asked me if we use a question mark after a reported question. I said, "No."

Calling from the beach, he asked for an extension on his paper. The teacher laughed at him and asked him if he was kidding—it was already a month late.

HOW TO BEAT THE SNOBS
Any Questions?

Before we get into the meat of beating the snobs, a quick story. Once upon a time, printers used to leave a space between the question and the question mark, and then they would leave a double space between the question mark and the next sentence. This is no longer a thing and should not happen. Do not do it. The end.

As an end-of-sentence punctuation point, the question mark is in direct conflict with the period and exclamation point. And it pips them both—especially when they are inside quotation marks.

> "Is this how you do it?" she asked.
>
> He asked, "We use questions marks inside the quotation marks, right?"

Notice the comma and the period disappear, and the question mark takes their place. All hail the question mark. Where the question mark goes in quotation marks, though, seems to cause problems with quite a few people—even the pedants. But it's all really quite simple. If the question mark is part of the quotation, the question mark stays inside the quotation marks. If the question mark involves the whole sentence, it sits outside the quotation marks:

> Mum asked, "Are you seriously wearing those?"
>
> Do you understand what Hamlet means by "A little more than kin and less than kind"?

Nor did his stepfather. #askingforafriend. No worries.

Rhetorical questions, too, are allowed out without a question mark; although, this is one of those uses without hard-and-fast rules. A rhetorical question is really more of a statement than a question and, like question tags, are a great way to get conversation moving. Sometimes a rhetorical question will start with a negative word to mean something positive:

Didn't the Crippses throw a cracking party?

or

Didn't the Crippses throw a cracking party.

And sometimes a rhetorical question will just sound like a question but not really expect an answer.

Why bother?

Guess what.

How about that?

Who cares.

Who knew?

Notice some of the examples above use question marks and some do not. That is because not using a question mark in a rhetorical question is really down to preference, but, like anything, it is important to stay consistent (yes, this is definitely a game of do as I say, not as I do).

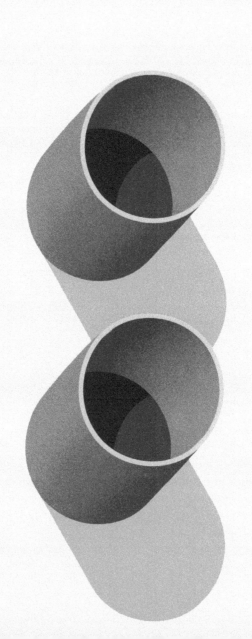

CHAPTER FIVE
THE COLON

The colon is quite the thinker, quite profound, never happy with all the superficial jibber-jabber that goes on these days. It tries to join in—it really does. It starts out quite light, quite general, but it just cannot take it anymore and in deep it goes. Getting all specific and detailed.

But it is not a crashing bore with its specifics and details. My English teacher called the colon "the mark of expectation or addition"—one of the few things I learned about grammar and punctuation at school. The colon is compelled to add explanation, to elaborate, and to share its learnings, and more often than not, it gives the sentence a nice change of pace to boot.

Far too many people—invariably the punctuation pedants who are trying to one-up everyone else just by using it—misuse it. Its similarity in look and name to the semicolon appears to have bamboozled the majority. The difference, though, is simple: The colon leads you onward in the sentence, taking you by the hand to a deeper understanding. The semicolon divides a sentence (more on that later).

To stand out from the crowd, learn to use the colon with elegance, and you will be perfectly placed to infiltrate the punctuation snobs and take them down from the inside.

Use to Set Off a List

The easiest way to use a colon is to put it after an independent clause and before a list.

> Things we still need for the Cripps party: bunting, cake, and someone to jump out of the cake.

Do keep your wits about you, though. Sticking a colon in when the list fits naturally into a sentence is a no-no in all style guides, with both AP and *The Blue Book* telling us not to use a colon after a verb:

> **For the Cripps party, we still need bunting, cake, and someone to jump out of the cake.**

Look! No colon. Spotted anything else? Say, the lack of capitals?

Because in a list that follows a colon, we do not use capitals. But in this internet day and age, we all know how much website visitors love their lists in bullet points because they are that much

MEMORY TIP
The Colon

There are loads of little ways to remember when and how to use a colon.

1. AP and the lawyers' *Blue Book* handily suggest never using a colon after a verb, preposition, or after "including."

> **WRONG** What I want to say is: I love punctuation
>
> **WRONG** I like everyone in my family, including: my children, my parents, and even my husband.
>
> **WRONG** The best way to get there is by: taking the train then walking a mile or so.

2. Think of the colon as taking a sentence from more general to more specific.

> **more general: more specific**

3. A little trick for formal letters:

> if your letter finishes with "sincerely," "faithfully," or "best regards," **use a colon**
>
> If "love," "from," or "yours" is at the end, **go with a comma**

There should be no hyphen after the colon (this monstrosity ":-"). If you should see it, remove it.

easier to read. Very kindly, *The Blue Book* lets us use capitals if our list is in bullet points. Thus.

> **Still needed for the Cripps party:**
> **· Bunting**
> **· Cake**
> **· Someone to jump out of the cake**

The chances are programs like Word or Pages or Google Docs, or whatever you use, will force you to cap up in a bullet list, anyway, so it is nice that at least one of the style guides gave us its blessing. Just always make sure you present colon bullet lists the same in each piece of writing.

Use to Introduce a Concept, Description, or Definition

We are on the beach. We have sunbathed, read a chapter of our book, and taken photos of our toes in the sand. We have chosen the best one (photo, not toe) and posted it online to infuriate friends back home. Now, it is time to explore.

Goggles in hand, we wade into the clear water. We pull the goggles over our eyes—here comes the metaphor (goggles=the colon)—we dip beneath the surface, and a world of fish, coral, and sand greets us. We are having an adventure.

That moment before we put our goggles on is the independent clause (it must be an independent clause before the colon). Putting the goggles over our eyes is the colon. And everything after the colon is the adventure, the description, the definition. It is everything we are here for.

To put it more simply, a colon takes writing from more general to more specific. It digs us down into what we really want to say; it takes us beneath the surface.

> Social media is so important: Without it, how would everyone know how happy we are?

> Hanging out at the beach is amazing: the sea, the fish, the colons.

> When parents say "faster," it can mean only one thing: cross the road.

Before the colon, we need an independent clause. After the colon, we can use a single word, a list, a phrase, a dependent clause, or another independent clause (the arguments about capitals after a colon are rife; we will get to them later).

Use Before a Block of Quoted Text

Remember all the way back in the comma chapter, there was this tip:

Quick note: If your quotation takes up more than two lines or is longer than two sentences, you introduce it with a colon, not a comma. (See the chapter on colons.)

Well, here we are, in the colon chapter.

When we borrow other people's beautifully composed words, we use either a comma or a colon to introduce the quoted text. While the comma is strong enough to introduce single-sentence quotations, only the colon is capable and strong enough to control quoted text more than two sentences long.

HOW TO BEAT THE SNOBS
Capital Usage

Those two little vertical dots have just one use: to show that what is coming explains, defines, or elaborates on what came before. But colons catch many people out. Not least, the punctuation pedants, who have huddled around the colon as if it were punctuation aristocracy; they fawn on it, often misuse it, and make everyone else feel nervous about it.

One of the main battles is how to use capitals with the colon. Each style guide has its own take on the caps rule, but they all agree lists and dependent clauses after a colon do not use caps, unless they are words we capitalize anyway.

> Words we cap up after a colon: table and chair, NO, but Lucy and Chicago, YES.

For bullet-pointed lists, we can either use caps or not. What a giddy choice.

> This is a list with capitals after the colon:
> · One word
> · Two words

If these bullets were in a horizontal, non-bulleted list, they would not have caps:

> This is a list with lowercase words after the colon: one word, two words.

All very easy.

It's with independent clauses that things get trickier, thanks to the style guides.

- **APA** and **AP** say use a capital to start any independent clause after the colon.

- **MLA** and **CMS** say use lowercase to start a single independent clause, but for multiple independent clauses, start the first with a capital.

- *Blue Book* essentially agrees with MLA and CMS but gives us the freedom to choose what we do with a single independent clause.

So choose your weapon and carry your colon with pride.

One of my favorite quotes from the granddaddy of great quotes Oscar Wilde: "Most people are other people. Their thoughts are someone else's opinions, their lives a mimicry, their passions a quotation."

Which might not be the most scientific or academic quotation ever, but both MLA and APA as well as CMS expect to see colons, like this, before longer quotations.

For CMS, the colon also uses its strength to add emphasis in dialogue or shorter quotations.

> **But one Oscar Wilde corker still valid today: "Be yourself; everyone else is already taken."**

While we are looking at colons in formal writing—the science and academic stuff—we should quickly drop by formal business letters. After the salutation (the "Dear"), in formal business letters, we use a colon before launching into our important business.

> Dear Sir or Madam:

> Dear Mrs. President:

But if our letter is less formal, a comma is perfectly acceptable:

> Dear Oscar,

> Dear Dad,

CHAPTER SIX
THE SEMICOLON

The semicolon. There he is. Bow down. We have
***Indiana Jones**ed our way through the Temple of*
Doom, raided lost Arks, and crawled through pits of
punctuation marks to find the Holy Grail of
punctuation understanding. Lo! He is before us.

The semicolon. What a moment! But, from the other side of
the cave (of course it is a cave, this is the end of a fierce quest . . .
there is always a cave), all we hear are the raucous giggles of
the winking semicolon, sitting on a rock, head thrown back as he
shakes with laughter, pointing at us in deep amusement.

"Why do you mock us, oh, semicolon?"

"Ahaha, because you're all silly sausages. How could you think I'm so difficult? I have two things to do. TWO. And you all think I'm so deep and complicated. Not a bit of it."

. . . and he carries on laughing and pointing at us.

What? So all that nonsense from the punctuation snobs, building the semicolon up to be some PhD punctuation mark, making us feel inferior, was all a ploy to put us off the scent. To give themselves a sense of superiority. Pah to them.

When I tell people what I do, it takes punctuation pedants about 8.3 seconds to crowbar their love of semicolons into the conversation. It is always the semicolon. Oh, how fond they are of semicolons. They use them all the time, don't you know?

But you know who does not love semicolons? Everyone else.

Use in a Punctuated List

Using the semicolon in a punctuated list is possibly where semicolon's power has come from. There are a lot of people who call him the "super-comma," which gives him an inflated sense of self-importance.

But why "super-comma"? Well, because he separates lists that have other punctuation in them, giving each element in the list a little more space. When there are loads of commas, colons, and em dashes flying around in a list, things can get pretty heated.

> The delegates are Lucy Cripps, Elle Woods, Harvard University, Captain Blackadder, University of Life.

The Semicolon

"What happened to the semicolon that broke the grammar laws?"

"It was given two consecutive sentences."

This little gem caused quite the ripple of giggles in one of the classes I taught, years ago.

What with that and my overactive imagination seeing the semicolon symbol (;) as Supercomma, cape flapping behind him as he shoots skyward to save badly punctuated lists from utter confusion, we can see semicolons as having two very clear tasks.

It's a shame there is so much nastiness around semicolon use; writers of considerable note have almost come to blows over it. There have even been calls to end it completely.

Noted author Kurt Vonnegut had an apparent dislike of semicolons that was legendary; semicolons, elsewhere, have been likened to disused cherry pitters (Ben Dolnick, *New York Times*); a tick on a dog's belly (author Donald Barthelme); and punctuation's axis of evil (Trevor Butterworth, *Financial Times*).

Yet style guides have remarkably little to say about them. So please, spend some time with the semicolon, and you just might learn to love the cheeky little so-and-so.

Say what? That is a lot of delegates—and some appear to be entities rather than humans—how do we cater to them!?

In strolls semicolon, with his big old cape and ill-fitting tights to settle between each element of the list, and things do, to be fair to him, get a lot easier to read.

> **The delegates are Lucy Cripps; Elle Woods, Harvard University; Captain Blackadder, University of Life.**

Ah, well, grammatically that makes more sense now. We maybe should not question the reality of it all.

Use to Connect Related Thoughts

Despite its childish arrogance about having superpowers, the semicolon is also quite thoughtful, sharing its ability to separate (or connect) two closely related independent clauses. It is especially fond of helping coordinating conjunctions and conjunction adverbs and has crafted itself a sweet little role that gives them a bit of time off.

Remember the FANBOYS (the coordinating conjunctions, **for, and, nor, but, or, yet, so**) back in the comma chapter? Remember they sit with a comma between two independent clauses? Well, semicolon has generously said it will stand in, so they can all go out together.

> Semicolon is very fond of his conjunction friends, **so** he has told the FANBOYS to take the night off.
>
> Semicolon is stepping in for the FANBOYS, **but** they will be back tomorrow.

And here is what the sentences look like with semicolon standing in.

> **Semicolon is very fond of his conjunction friends; he has told the FANBOYS to take the night off.**
>
> **Semicolon is stepping in for the FANBOYS; they will be back tomorrow.**

The semicolon takes the place of both the comma and the conjunction.

This same thing happens with conjunction adverbs (however, therefore, thus, etc.) and words that set up examples (that is, for example, you know, etc.). When you see these words, check what function they are playing before sprinkling semicolons around. If they are single phrases making an aside comment, they do not have a semicolon. If they sit before an independent clause, they do.

> Some sentences need a semicolon; however, other sentences do not.
>
> This sentence, however, does not need a semicolon.

HOW TO BEAT THE SNOBS
Semicolon vs. Colon

People use semicolons, according to Kurt Vonnegut, to try to look better than the rest of us. More educated. More knowledgeable. But the pedants so often get it wrong in their hurry to outwit us blockheads and, in the process, make themselves look wonderfully dimwitted. As a result, there is general lack of understanding about semicolons, which has led to distrust, dislike, and discrimination. Bloody semicolons, coming over here, punctuating our sentences, giving us pause, building effect.

One of the most common semicolon misunderstandings is muddling them with colons.

The rule of the semicolon connecting two related thoughts can very easily slip into colon territory. When writing, consider whether the two sentences are closely connected ideas or if the second one elaborates on the first (which is a job for colon).

See here:

> Working from home is great for life-work balance.
>
> Catching up on Netflix over lunch is a particular perk.
>
> **Working from home is great for life-work balance; catching up on Netflix over lunch is a particular perk.**

Clearly a case for the semicolon.

Whereas, see how the second half of this sentence elaborates on why France is a wonderful country.

> **France is a wonderful country: The wine is divine, the cheese is delicious, and the people are very friendly.**

Sometimes it can be difficult to decide, but practice makes . . . a bit better.

Oh, and by the way, never use a semicolon before any of the FANBOYS, and never, ever use a capital after a semicolon (unless it's a proper noun, of course).

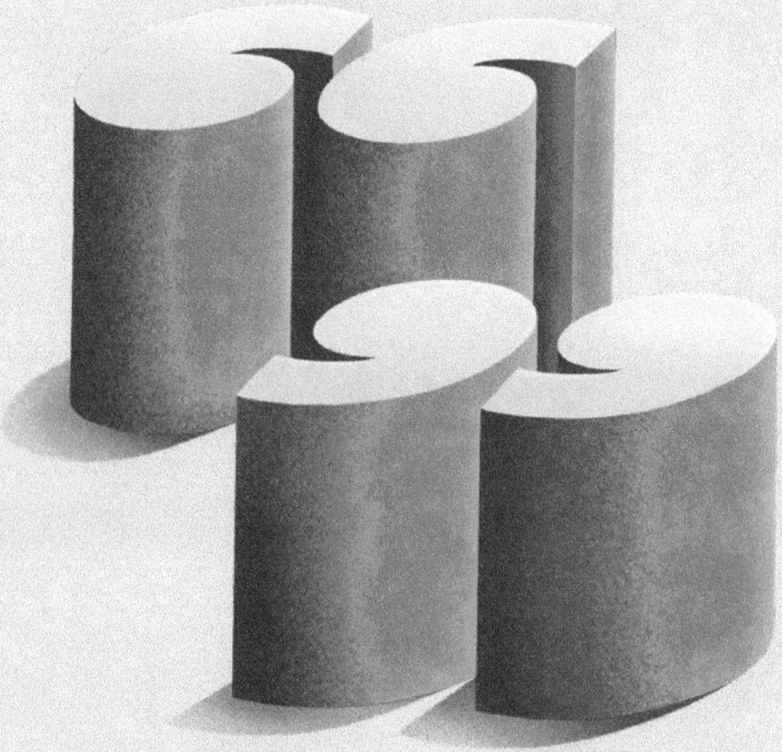

CHAPTER SEVEN

THE QUOTATION MARK

Scare quotes. Air quotes. Speech marks. Inverted commas. Quote marks. Quotation marks. These little 66–99 double acts have more aliases than Jason Bourne. But there is nothing mysterious here. Nothing to hide.

In their pairs, quotation marks have a solid collection of uses that, for the most part, all style guides agree to and follow consistently. Quotation marks' main role is to frame either direct speech or a quotation that absolutely nails what we want to say. Think of them as the jazz hands that show we have reserved the honor of quotation marks for a truly blow-away quotation. Because quoting someone means, sure, we like what they have said, but, most importantly, we love how they have said it.

So quotation marks are obviously for quotations and direct speech, yes. But they have some other jobs, too: to show irony, to explain the meaning or unusual use of a word, and to pick out titles.

How? We open the quotation marks at the beginning of our "quoted, ironic, unusual, defined word, phrase, or sentence," and close the quotation marks after it. That is all.

Use to Set Off a Quotation or Direct Speech

Quotations present exactly the words as they are in the original. No changes. And whether we want to quote someone else's entire comment or just pick out a single word or phrase, we use quotation marks to show these are not our words, but we are pretty impressed by them.

> My favorite quote of all time is from Oscar Wilde, who said, "I can resist everything except temptation."

We also use quotation marks in direct speech and creative dialogue. When we do this, each piece of dialogue by one person has its own quotation marks and its own line. Drop a line every time a new person speaks.

> Everyone was happy until the barkeep shouted, "Last call at the bar, please, then drink up and get outta here." He ruined the evening.

But we do not use quotation marks in he-said-she-said (indirect) speech, like this:

> He said it was last call at the bar, and we all needed to finish our drinks. He ruined the evening.

When a quotation or one-person speech continues beyond a single paragraph, we keep the quotation marks open at the end of the first paragraph and only close the quotation marks at the end of the whole quotation:

> "Paragraph one.
>
> "Paragraph two.
>
> "Third and final paragraph."

For longer quotations, we can use block quotations—those big indented chunks of quotation we see in academic writing. They have no quotation marks; the indent shows it is a quotation and not part of our own writing.

Use to Show Irony

These are scare quotes. They remind us of that "hilarious" joke Drunk Uncle Bob cracked before toppling into the pool, and everyone "made their excuses" and left the party, at top speed.

We see people physically create scare quotes when they use their index and middle fingers on both hands to add "quotes," "irony," or "emphasis" to their speech. These are air quotes, and, yes, they are annoying. But we have to love the scare-air pun, right?!

But we should be clear about what irony is, quickly. Irony is saying the opposite of what we mean, for emphasis or comic effect. So, it turns out, Drunk Uncle Bob's joke was really not hilarious—it was awful enough for people to find reasons to leave the party without mentioning Drunk Uncle Bob's horrific behavior.

Unfortunately, way too many people (*ahem, pedants) use quotation marks to add emphasis to words, but using quotation marks to add emphasis is not a thing, so those people end up sounding ridiculous.

> We'd like to say a big "thank you" to all our customers who have "supported" us over the years. We are now closed.

Yeah, like, really, thanks. Thanks for nothing.

> Please order your "food" and "drinks" at the bar.

Do nothing at the bar and leave. Ordering "food" or "drink" anywhere here is not going to end well. Leave immediately.

So do be careful with sprinkling quotation marks around willy-nilly—get it wrong, and the joke is on you.

Use to Explain the Meaning or Unusual Use of a Real or Made-up Word

When we use an unusual word in an unusual way, it is wise to show our reader we know what we are doing. It distances us from the word. We are telling the reader, yes, we know this is not how the word is usually used, but there is this other meaning or odd use of the word you might like to know about.

> When my friend answered the cell, she said she was "passengering"—which I took to mean she wasn't driving.

> I'm not used to all this corporate speak. It took me ages to work out what "have the bandwidth to drill down" meant and unpick "put a couple more builds in the pipeline."

> When my son was very little, he insisted on doing things on his "rown," after we asked him, "Do you want to do it on your own?"

Letting him do things on his rown as a teenager is definitely easier.

All style guides agree that unusual words, slang, jargon, and made-up words should have quotation-mark frames, but when we talk about a word as a word, the style guides part ways.

News crews discussing a word as a word use quotation marks around that word.

> The phrase "faster" does not, in fact, mean "cross the road."

The other styles put that word in italics.

> The phrase *faster* does not, in fact, mean "cross the road."

As with anything, there is too much of a good thing. A page littered with quotation marks is daunting and distracting, so keep them in check.

How to Use Single Quotation Marks

Relatively new to the quotation-mark family, single quotation marks do exactly the same as regular quotations, but inside other

HISTORY LESSON
The Quotation Mark

Time for another trip back to ancient Greece. This time for a quotation-mark history lesson at the Library of Alexandria, circa 2 B.C. Famous for saying loads of important stuff, the ancient Greeks used a little mark called a diple to draw attention to what they thought was the most important. You know, pithy remarks, pat-on-the-back moments, something challenging, something worthy of comment. A bit like how we use quotation marks today.

Not wanting the ancient Greeks to take all the credit, medieval scribes, copying clerical papers, drew attention to the scriptures by colorfully underlining or decorating them. Maybe that is the inspiration for the modern motivational quote—you know, the ones presented on a picture of a wide-open plain, deserted beach, or vast mountainous landscape.

When printing first evolved, underlining in color was not especially practical, so early printers looked to the Greeks' diple. There has been some backing and forwarding by punctuation historians over the years, but the earliest use of modern-looking quotation marks seems to be around the late 15th century/early 16th century, not all that long after Gutenberg handed the world his history-changing printing press.

And much like today's overeager punctuationalists, early printers scattered quotation marks everywhere, putting one at the beginning of every line of the quotation. They calmed down eventually, keeping quotation marks just to the beginning and end of the quotation.

It was not until the 1800s that single quotation marks emerged to identify a quotation within a quotation. But while the Americans have always used double quotation marks with single quotations inside the quotation, the Brits have done—and continue to do—the exact opposite.

quotations. They are the second-level frame. The auxiliary quotation marks when the double-marks are already busy.

> "If you want a pacific engraving on your iPhone, something like 'Mom's iPhone,' please write it on this sheet."

> "Did you say 'pacific'? Do you mean 'specific'?"

> "Yes, write it on here."

. . . one week later

> "Hi, I just picked up my new iPhone, but you have engraved 'I don't want my iPhone engraved' on it. I specifically said I didn't want an engraving."

Fun fact: Over the pond, the Brits flip how they use single and double quotation marks. So, for them, single quotation marks do most of the work, and the double quotation marks just cover the in-quotation quotation work.

How to Use Quotation Marks or Italics in Titles

Most styles—except news outlets—use italics for main titles and quotation marks for the little parts that make up the whole: the chapters, the articles, the poems, the episodes.

When we use quotation marks for anything in the right column of the chart on the next page, we put them around the element we are referring to, taking care not to add in other elements of the title or sentence.

I really enjoyed reading Dickens' *The Pickwick Papers* at school, but my favorite chapter by a long way was "Too full of adventure to be briefly described." We need more chapter titles like that.

When the Civil War finally finished, the *New York Herald* ran a story simply titled "The End."

ITALICS	QUOTATION MARKS
Book titles	Chapter titles, short-story titles
Magazine and newspaper names	Newspaper and magazine article titles
TV show names	Episode titles
Music album titles	Song titles
Pieces of art	Poems

And while the rest of us are trying to remember what needs quotation marks and what needs italics, the news outlets are sitting pretty, using quotation marks for everything except religious and reference books.

HOW TO BEAT THE SNOBS
Stick to the Rules

We all know how to use quotation marks. There really is nothing complicated or mysterious about them, but somehow, someone has managed to create discombobulating oddities to bamboozle and confuse us.

Maybe that was the plan.

But the best way to beat the snobs is to just get it right. To not sprinkle quotation marks around wherever. To not try emphasizing words with quotation marks. To not add random other punctuation to proceedings.

Just remember:

> **Commas and periods are almost always inside the closing quotation mark.**

Colons and semicolons are always placed outside the closing quotation mark.

> **Question marks and exclamation points go either inside or outside the quotation marks, depending on whether the question or exclamation is part of the quotation (in which case it goes inside) or part of the sentence (outside).**

If the quotation is a complete sentence, it begins with a capital letter.

> According to Mark Twain, "Travel is fatal to prejudice, bigotry, and narrow-mindedness."

If the quotation simply flows into the rest of the sentence, the quotation takes no capital.

> Mark Twain told the audience that "travel is fatal to prejudice, bigotry, and narrow-mindedness."

Above all else, remember that quotation marks around a word, unless we are very clearly talking about that word, just sound sarcastic. After all, who wants to be the fireworks "you can trust" or the "real" plastic surgeon of the punctuation world?

CHAPTER EIGHT

THE EXCLAMATION MARK

When it comes to exclamation points, my daughter's friend possesses that wonderful perception only children seem to have: "Children's books have loads of exclamation points, but there are fewer and fewer in books as we get older."

Her dad mused that maybe the older we get, the less surprised we are by everything—less shocked, less astonished, less angered, and less disgusted, so we have less need for exclamation points.

The Exclamation Point

There is a rather wonderful story that has the exclamation point as the love child of the i and the o of the Latin word io, an exclamation of happiness or success. Word on the street suggests that medieval scribes (yes, them again) used io at the end of an especially joyful sentence, and, over time, the space-precious copyists moved the i above the o to create our exclamation point.

Also, there are notions that suggest it is as old as cave paintings, as the pyramids, as the ancient Greeks. But no one seems entirely sure.

What is certain, though, is enthusiasm for the enthusiastic attention seeker does not seem to be waning, with social posts and emails littered with exclamation marks. Why?

Maybe, as the Netflix show *Explained*, suggested, exclamation points have a recent history of being flashy, used in women's novels and comic books and by show-off advertisers. They are morphing into a show of friendliness, of excitement or frustration, of being kind—none of which scream "I'm professional."

But currently, the exclamation point is too much at home in gossipy celeb magazines. It is the selfie of the punctuation world, drawing attention to itself and whatever it thinks is hilarious or shocking enough to comment on, which, it seems, is nearly everything. It has become excitable, vacuous, and altogether self-absorbed.

We need to call time on this skittish, high-spirited use of the exclamation point and return it to its intended use. The abuse has gone on long enough.

In the vast majority of writing—in science papers, academic publications, business writing, and news reporting—exclamation points really have no place. At best, they belong in informal fiction, dialogue comic books, and sensational commentary. Used correctly, they can build a dramatic moment, heighten tension, and make quite a point, but, as with everything, the more they are used, the less impact they have.

Use to Exclaim

Put the exclamation point after a single word or short phrase to show strong feeling, great emotion, or a surprised reaction that starts with **how** or **what**.

> What big teeth you have!
>
> How lovely!
>
> Boo!
>
> Stop!

In prose, the exclamation point replaces the period, and, in dialogue it sits next to its phrase; that might mean it goes inside or outside the quotation marks.

She squealed, "Those shoes are gorg. Just, wow!"

How nice of her to say "you are wonderful hosts" before leaving!

Warning: What comes next might upset you.

When those little single words—**oh, wow, goodness**—start a sentence, though, we do not need an exclamation point.

Oh, I love those shoes.

Wow, that dress is next-level gorgeous.

Desperately hunting around for an exclamation point? Feeling underdressed? Struggling to breathe?

It does take time, but you can reduce exclamation points in your life, and feel all the more grown-up for it. Exclamation points are shouty, so the less we use them, the less shouty and more serene we are.

See the difference between

Oh, shut up.

Oh, shut up!

The first one, without the exclamation point, is playful, quiet, said to a friend in warmth and jest. But that second one? It is furious. It is at the end of its tether. It cannot hear another. Flipping. Word.

Notice, also, that all the examples use just one exclamation point. Not one of them throws their head back in guffaws and staccato shoots out exclamation point after exclamation point. One is plenty.

HOW TO BEAT THE SNOBS
Break the Habit

Snobbery surrounds exclamation points. Punctuation purists have seen them as flighty, perky, and just a bit childish. But when the digital age brought multiple exclamation points into our lives, something had to give.

I was once an exclamation point abuser—part of the rise of the digital age in the early noughties, when exclamation points moved from being less "overused" and more "abused." I would send emails with multiple exclamation points—excited by my own wit and my own weak jokes.

But I had an epiphany early in my lecturing career and put my days of exclamation abuse behind me. If you are happy to continue using exclamation points to make a show of friendliness, go for it. If you want to join me on the less-exclamationy side of the fence, here is my advice to you.

Do not try to go cold turkey. Start by limiting yourself to three exclamation points a day for a week, then two for the following week. By the third week, drop to one a day. By my one-a-day week, I had already broken the habit. But maybe I was one of the lucky ones.

Slowly but surely, we will say goodbye to exclamation-point abuse. Soon, hopefully, every social post, every email, every blog will no longer be riddled with multiple exclamation points and move to a more serene, measured tone.

CHAPTER NINE
THE HYPHEN

Half-pint hyphen is stronger than he looks. He pulls together two or more words to create one meaning, and in doing so, kicks confusion to the curb. Or at least that is the plan.

Look at the difference between a "small business owner" and a "small-business owner." What about "fast dog food delivery service"? What is going on? "Fast-dog food-delivery service"? "Fast dog-food delivery service"? Despite doing a lot of the donkey work in keeping writing sensical, the hyphen is being hunted. Heavyweights from Winston Churchill to, it seems, the Oxford English Dictionary, want to rid writing of this helpful little chap.

In 2007, the Oxford English Dictionary kicked out 16,000 hyphens. "Well-being," gone. "Bumble-bee," gone. "Test-tube," no more. "Ice-cream," bye-bye now. They are now either two words (ice cream, test tube, and fig leaf), or one word (bumblebee, website, email). Why did this happen? Well, because people have stopped using them; "Because they're confusing," whines everyone, everywhere.

Granted, they are one of the tougher punctuation marks to master. So the obvious advice would be consult a dictionary. Dictionaries know. Alas, dictionaries cannot agree on which words to join, separate, or hyphenate and which to leave alone. Unhelpful. Merriam-Webster and America Heritage dictionaries want a "waterbed," but OED wants a "water bed." *sigh

Before exploring hyphen's function, we need to talk looks. Because with hyphens, looks do matter. For clarity: Type the hyphen with no space either side, using that tiny line key on your keyboard or numpad (-). Hyphens are not dashes (—, –), and we will come to those on page 98.

Use to Join Compound Modifiers

Everyone has been to ceremonies where two words join to make a single compound adjective that describes a third word, right?

"We are gathered to celebrate the joining of these two words, Over and Easy, before Eggs. They put asunder all other words, and with this hyphen commit, heart and soul, to creating new meaning: over-easy eggs.

"Only before Eggs will they continue to share that meaning. Should they fall behind Eggs, they will be one no more, forgoing their hyphen, casting aside their matrimony, and, once again, be known as eggs over easy."

Quick AP sidenote: In the news world, hyphenated modifiers after the noun following "to be" can keep the hyphen. So, the steak is well-done, the eggs are over-easy, the children are injury-prone. APA and MLA never hyphenate post noun.

Ceremonial language can be hard to unpick, so allow me: We often use two or more words to add information to another, say "first class discussion" (there will be more), "60 odd people" (steer clear), and "toy robot business" (only for children) or, one of my favorites, "sparkling water dispenser" (how very glam).

Now try with hyphens.

> **First-class discussion**
>
> **60-odd people**
>
> **Toy-robot business**
>
> **Sparkling-water dispenser**

Ah, things become much clearer, if much less entertaining.

Logic really must play a part, though. When compounds are so well known that no one would misread them—think the "income tax returns," "real estate agents," and "high school teachers" of this world—we do without the hyphen. These are the hyphens Churchill et al. have a problem with. The unnecessary, the slightly patronizing, the excessive.

Quicker sidenote: There is never a hyphen after "-ly" adverbs, so a happily married couple is always just happily married. Never happily-married. Remember, "family" is a noun, so "family-run business" is fine.

Use to Join Compound Nouns

Compound nouns are two or more words pulled together to create a noun, like "commander-in-chief," "chocolate cake," "writer-illustrator." Now, because this is English, and we loathe easy, some compound nouns are hyphenated; some are not. And it all depends on our prescribed dictionary or style guide. Yes, once again, they have created all the confusion, pulling us this way and that. Everything is right. Everything is wrong.

Go deeper to see the vast differences in style guides and exception piled on exception. June Casagrande's *The Best Punctuation Book, Period* dedicates 26 glorious pages to our half-pint buddy— a great resource.

But our purpose here is to hold our own around punctuation snobs. The best way to do that is to place evidence, either from a dictionary or style guide, under a punctuation snob's nose. Yes, they can argue, but we are just as correct as they are.

Also playing in our favor is the speed at which new words evolve because only the pros can really keep up. Often new words start with two single words, then adopt a hyphen just before becoming single words. The more common the word, the quicker the evolution. Think **email, esports, website, notebook, laptop.**

When "email" was just coming out of diapers, I insisted on using "e-mail," as in "electronic-mail." But others used Email, E-mail, email. Chaos. By my reasoning that e- had to stay. What would happen when eentertainment, eevent, eedition, eeducation, eemployee came along? Just ridiculous. But, it seems, that is where we are heading. The hyphen after e is no more. Maybe we, too, must eevolve and eembrace it.

Use for Prefixes and Suffixes

As with all hyphens, checking a dictionary or style guide is definitely our first port of call in hyphenating prefixes and suffixes. Hyphens, here, are handy to avoid a stream of consonants or vowels (**"antiinflammatory"** and **"shelllike"** clearly need hyphens), to sidestep confusion ("re-cover" or "recover"?), and to prefix numbers ("pre-1990s," "post-2000") and capitalized words ("un-American," "pro-EU" but not White-House staff . . . just White House staff).

Not all prefixes and suffixes, by a long shot, need hyphens, but those that do, really do.

Compare

> She loved the recreation of her favorite childhood games.

with

> **She loved the re-creation of her favorite childhood games.**

and

> They recovered their grandma's best chairs.

with

They re-covered their grandma's best chairs.

Yes, they do make a difference, don't they?

All US style guides agree on a few other points, too:

"cooperate" and "coordinate" do not have a hyphen

Prefix "in-" has a hyphen (so, "in-depth report," "in-house copy editor." But use no hyphen when "in" means "not" (i.e., "incapable," "inaccurate," "indirect").

Suffixes in "president-elect," "doll-like," "half-full," and "100-odd" take hyphens, **but hyphens generally have no place near suffixes.**

If adding a prefix means we double- or triple-up on consonants or vowels, we use a hyphen to keep things neat. "Antiaircraft," for example, is a mess to read, as is "antiinflation," but "antibiotic" and "antifreeze" are perfectly fine.

Fundamentally, we need to be switched on when deciding whether to use hyphens or not and just keep our ears to the ground for major changes, like when "to-day" and "to-morrow" lost their hyphens. That is all.

HISTORY LESSON
The Hyphen

Thank you, Dionysius Thrax! Thank you for having a tremendous name and for giving us the hyphen, or the *hypó hén*—"under one." Dionysius Thrax—we must use his full name because it is too good to not—joined with his curved, below-the-line hyphen two words that were read as one. Just as we do today.

By the Middle Ages, scribes used the hyphen to tut at other copyists who had incorrectly written two words instead of one. They would draw a line to close the inaccurate space as the schmo who got it wrong sank lower on his stool.

Gutenberg, as he did with so many punctuation marks, took the hyphen to the masses. He painstakingly carved every letter and mark to make his printing look as handwritten as possible, but he was unable to alter the size of his letters and spaces to justify his work, so he hyphenated words to split them over two lines—as we still do in printed writing.

Slowly but surely, the hyphen has fallen out of favor. *The New York Times* said goodbye to its hyphenated masthead in the 1890s, and, in 1945, members of the New York City Council tried to outlaw hyphenating New York as a compound noun. Today, the fanatically dogged New-York Historical Society retains its hyphen and even fields the Hyphens softball team.

HOW TO BEAT THE SNOBS
Suspensive Hyphenation

Namaste! Welcome to the pool of suspensive hyphenation, where words, connected or alone, drift with their hyphen. Float, relax. Ohm shanti.

See, "sisters-" floating with its hyphen, apparently with no other word. But it is aware its partner is suspended in its own hyphenation, nearby, with the noun they both fundamentally change.

There, "and brothers-in-law." See that invisible thread between them, their unspoken bond: "sisters- and brothers-in-law."

Right. Ohm shanti your way out of that pool and join us on the loungers. What is going on here?

With a regular compound modifier, two words join to add meaning to their noun. Like this:

> **When the community-supported farm opened, everyone literally got a piece of the pie.**

All fine, there. Now, what if everyone in the community maintains the farm, too? Would we say, "When the community-supported and community-maintained farm opened . . ."? No. Get outta here. We would lose the second "community." Same in writing.

Hello, **suspensive hyphenation**. We add a hyphen to the other word that shares the noun.

> When the community-supported and -maintained farm opened . . .

Ta-daa!

But what happens if those anti-hyphenators (I made that up) got their way? This:

> When the community supported and maintained farm opened . . .

When we start to read that second sentence, without the hyphens, we naturally see "supported" and "maintained" as verbs, which messes with our heads, forcing us to reread.

Not ideal.

Suspensive hyphenation is pretty flexi. Choose a "community-supported and -maintained farm" or a "school- or home-based education." But as with all hyphenation, only use it when not using it messes with your chakras.

Namaste!

COMMON USES OF HYPHENS

COMPOUND NOUNS	EXAMPLE SENTENCE
Mother-in-law	Bravely, she invited her mother-in-law for dinner just days after the wedding.
L-shaped	Her favorite sofa is L-shaped, perfect for stretching out on.
Pay-as-you-go	Rather than getting a contract, I prefer to pay-as-you-go.
Two-thirds	Use of the education app dropped by two-thirds over the summer break.
Break-in	The kids found it hard to sleep again after the break-in.
Self-esteem	Her self-esteem improved when she did well in the pop quiz.

PREFIXES/SUFFIXES	EXAMPLE SENTENCE
Ex-husband	Her new husband and her ex-husband got on pretty well.
Self-imposed	She enjoyed her self-imposed weekend phone ban.
Semi-conscious	Semi-conscious, she answered the phone when it rang at 3 am.
Post-2008	House prices plummeted post-2008.
Non-violent	The organizers insisted it should be a non-violent protest.
60-odd	We invited 60-odd friends to the party and had an incredible night.

COMPOUND MODIFIERS	EXAMPLE SENTENCE
20-year-old woman	The 20-year-old woman wowed the audience with her portrayal of Lady Macbeth.
Well-written resume	The manager complimented her on the well-written resume.
Hard-working teachers	Hollyoaks High had great results thanks to the hard-working teachers.
Small-business manager	The small-business manager helped the couple start up their new enterprise.
Life-threatening illness	If caught in time, even life-threatening illnesses can be cured.
Snow-covered driveway	Shoveling the snow-covered driveway took nearly two hours.
Far-reaching ideas	In the meeting, her far-reaching ideas got her kudos from the management team.
Full-time job	This was his first full-time job out of school.
Good-looking unicorns	Good-looking unicorns are not great at tap dancing. Fact.
Up-to-date information	At the Unicorn Dancing Academy, we keep up-to-date information on all our students.

CHAPTER TEN
THE EM AND EN DASH

While the em dash is having a renaissance, shouting its thoughts, generally being opinionated and dramatic, the mild-mannered en dash is all but banished to the book-publishing world, rarely seen beyond printed pages.

Twice the width of a hyphen, the em dash is the width of, yes, an "m." Thus "—." (Although American lawyer Matthew Butternick says it is actually the width of an H.) Anyway. Presumably, you are ahead of me, but for the sake of balance, the en dash is the width of the printed "n." Like this, "–."

There are two ways to create em and en dashes.

> One, let the computer do it by typing **word+hyphen+hyphen+word** (word--word) for the em dash
>
> and **word+space+hyphen+hyphen+space+word** (word -- word) for the en dash, and it will autocorrect to the right length (remove the spaces around the en dash).

And, two, for an entertainingly smug thing to do near your resident snob, why not whip out a keyboard shortcut?

> Em dash (–): **Alt+0151**
>
> En dash (–): **Alt+0150**

Or even go with the Unicode numbers, **em dash 8212** and **en dash 8211**.

Neither dash has white space around it; they both snuggle up to the words around them. (If writing has space on either side of the dash, it is probably a Brit's doing.)

OK, we have spent quite a bit of time on how the dashes look and how to format them, but that is because so many people go wrong, choosing to just chuck a hyphen in for sort-of good measure. This is our time to shine.

Use the Em Dash for Sentence Breaks and Finales

Em dashes kick the comma, parentheses, colon, and semicolon out to add its own emphasis, mid-sentence or as an all-singing finale. It brings explanation, commentary, opinion, wit—the writer's voice.

The em dash takes our reader closer to our thoughts and gives writing a conversational, intimate quality that—let's face it—none of the other punctuation marks can.

> **We spent ages arranging the surprise party for Mom—then Dad ruined the whole thing, saying he'd see us later.**

Done well, the em dash can add panache, complexity, and vigor to writing. Overdone, though, and it becomes rude and interruptive, distracting the reader from the main point of the sentence and making the writer come over as chaotic, ditzy.

We must use em-dash power wisely, not wield it like a great sword. Carry it with a light grip that impresses the reader and leaves no question of who is in charge.

> When the teacher saw all the mistakes (no one in the class answered more than one question correctly), he handed the paper back and told everyone to try again.

> **When the teacher saw all the mistakes—no one in the class answered more than one question correctly—he handed the paper back and told everyone to try again.**

See how those parentheses help us feel the teacher's quiet desperation, his tolerance, and his hope that next time—just maybe—they will get it right. With em dashes, not so much. They shift our focus and make us a bit furious; we tut and roll our eyes at the class.

Just quickly, note how the em dash barges the comma—and the parenthesis or colon—out of the way.

Use the Em Dash for Important Lists

The em dash also sets up all manner of lists. Lists quickly thrown together mid-sentence. Lists of important items or people that need to work in apposition to another noun. A list that needs to be part of the sentence because we want to say more after it. Sometimes, these lists are more frantic or annoyed than the rather-more-genteel colon list; other times, they give the attention deserved by the elements in the list.

Remember Dad ruined the surprise party? Adding a list really brings home the frustration while keeping the items near the "everything" that refers to them and getting get rid of the colon, so it is much tidier.

> **We had planned everything for the surprise party—the balloons, the cake, all the relatives coming into town—then Dad blew it all, saying he'd see us later.**

Try to make this sentence work as well with a colon or loads of commas, instead. Dare you.

Now imagine we are writing a list about something or someone very important. How would they feel if we stuck them in parentheses?

> The royalty of late-night satire (Seth Meyers and Samantha Bee, John Oliver and Trevor Noah) bring the news to millennials.

It just seems like we are hiding them away—they deserve more than just commas or brackets. We would probably all feel a bit better doing this:

> **The royalty of late-night satire—Seth Meyers and Samantha Bee, John Oliver and Trevor Noah—bring the news to millennials.**

Having them mid-sentence keeps them front and center, where tacking them on the end, after a colon, would feel like, well, tacking them on the end.

Use the En Dash to Show Range

Remember the en dash is a very different creature to its shouty sibling. Smaller, far less used, and with only a couple of very specific uses. One of those is to avoid having to write **"to," "through,"** and **"until"** because, quite frankly, they all take just too much time. This is where the often maligned en dash pops in to help out.

> **We're catching the San Francisco–New York red-eye tonight.**
>
> **Our shindig runs 4:30–midnight.**
>
> **President Reagan (1911–2004) was in office 1981–1989.**

In using en dashes like this, we show there is a relationship between these two elements, but we are choosing not to use any range-type words, so we would not say

> Our shindig runs **from** 4:30–midnight.

MEMORY TIP
Em and En Dashes

Right off the bat, we need to be one hundred percent clear—the dash is NOT a hyphen. Remember that.

While the en dash is a nifty mark to have in your corner, and great for thwarting the snobs, the em dash is a must if you want to really take control of your writing. It has great power, visually, and is the shoutiest punctuation point we have. Master the em dash, and we go straight to the punctuation head table.

So what do we need to remember about en dash? Think of it as a big "SIS," supporting, helping out, helping us cut unnecessary words when we just want the low-down on dates, times, and ranges.

Shows an equal relationship

It's a super-hypen, pulling together two already-hyphenated compounds

Shows ranges of distance and time

And what about the em dash? Well, em dash "ADDs," emphasizes, and altogether makes a song and dance.

Adds punch to the end of a sentence

Draws attention to important lists

Draws attention to comments, opinions, and witticism

With em dash's general emotion, we are best to play it cool. Some advice suggests we use no more than two em dashes per paragraph; other advice recommends using it once or twice in a whole piece of writing. Editors recommend against overusing it, but, ironically, often overuse it while imparting that advice.

Do as they say, not as they do. The best advice with em dashes is to keep "em" in check—pun intended.

or

President Reagan (1911–2004) was in office **between** 1981–1989.

Oh no. Look away.

Used properly, see how the en dash just helps to keep that flow, without making the reader think these words are joined. The en dash gives its neighbors equal balance and equal importance, and gives the speaker space to add their own "and," should they want. At the same time, it does not take up unnecessary real estate for the silent reader. It really is very accommodating.

Use the En Dash for Multiword Compounds

This is a good one to have in our back pocket when the punctuation snob comes calling. So few people use the en dash correctly—if at all—that we can absolutely own it.

Take a bit of time to grasp its glorious effects on multiword hyphenated compounds, and just wait for your mic-drop moment.

We might like to show off by nonchalantly using an en dash to connect a prefix to an open compound (one without hyphens).

In the pre–Harry Potter world, children simply didn't read.

Fashion post–World War II changed considerably for women.

And when we want to show that two things share equal weighting, and there is a balance in their relationship, once again we turn to en dash.

They have a strong mother–daughter relationship.

Will we ever be able to cross the iPhone–Android divide?

How about that US–UK special relationship?

The en dash is also a kind of a big-brother hyphen. When we have two hyphenated compounds that we want to connect, en dash strides in, happy to help.

Grandpa's funeral was a half-happy–half-sad affair.

When the half-stumbling–half-walking toddler tumbled, we tried not to giggle.

See the difference in width between the hyphen (-) and the en dash (–)?

OK, we are ready. Go out and take the punctuation stage. Go ahead, you have got this.

HOW TO BEAT THE SNOBS
Use Em Dash Wisely

Em dash usurps commas, parentheses, colons, and semicolons at will, even when they are doing a bang-up job all on their own.

Maybe the most informal of all of them, the em dash gives writing a conversational, opinionated flavor, which rarely works in business, science, and academic writing. Use only, with incredible finesse, to replace another punctuation mark to make the perfect point.

Replace a comma

> Leo, playing accordion, and his band covered a classic 1980s synth-rock hit.
>
> **Leo—playing accordion—and his band covered a classic 1980s synth-rock hit.**

A what? An accordion in synth-rock? What next—a cowbell? The comma, here, is little more than a speed bump.

Replace a semicolon

> Kitty's soccer team is impressive; they are fierce girls, giving the other teams a good run for their money.
>
> **Kitty's soccer team is impressive—they are fierce girls, giving the other teams a good run for their money.**

So they really do sound fierce. I need to see these ladies play. Meanwhile, the semicolon slows that excitement down.

Replace a colon

> One thing everyone can do to make the world a better place: be kind.
>
> **One thing everyone can do to make the world a better place—be kind.**

Colon? Hello? We need more of a pause. Thank you, em dash.

Replace parentheses

> J.R.R. Tolkein's first novel (*The Hobbit*) was a remarkable success.
>
> **J.R.R. Tolkein's first novel—*The Hobbit*—was a remarkable success.**

Sorry, is this a joke? *The Hobbit* was his first novel?! Parentheses, stop whispering, speak up.

CHAPTER ELEVEN
THE PARENTHESIS AND THE BRACKET

Parentheses are curved brackets ( )—like hands cupped around a mouth, whispering to the reader, helping the reader with an explanation, a definition, a muttered comment.

Parentheses also contain pithy asides from the writer—kind of a direct line to their inner thoughts and opinions. What is inside those parentheses is not essential to the grammatical structure of the sentence, but it certainly creates a little safe space that keeps everyone on the same page.

Overused, parentheses become the hammy Shakespearean actor, stage left, right hand up to the mouth, eyes fixed on the audience as he wails and laments his character's erstwhile demise while everyone else on stage pretends to be oblivious to the drama.

Square brackets [ ], meanwhile, could not be less dramatic if they tried. More ordered, they line things up to make sure everything is clear, understood, A-OK. Writer says "he," bracket steps in to clarify who "he" is. Writer boldly uses a crazy-complicated, jargony word, bracket tips its hat, edges forward, and gives a quick definition or explanation. No judgment. No comment. Just honest-to-goodness service to make sure the reader stays abreast of the writer.

It is fair to say that no matter how pithy or useful parentheses or brackets are, if we can avoid using them, we really must. Overuse euthanizes good writing, making it a battle every step of the way through the sentence.

Use Parentheses to Set Off Helpful, but Not Vital Info, or Go Off on a Tangent

One parenthesis, two parentheses. A pair of parentheses. The opening parenthesis, the closing parenthesis. Two. Always two. Always.

Right, we have that sorted. But what do they do? Simply put, parentheses add opinion, boldish interruptions, snippets of facts, tidbits of information, a bit of ooh and ahh to proceedings without messing with the rest of the sentence.

Remove that information and we lose comment or definition, but we do not lose the sentence (see what I mean?).

Remove that information and we lose comment or definition, but we do not lose the sentence.

Generally speaking, we could also use either commas or dashes to add the same extra information, but by choosing to use parentheses, we dip our toes in the pool of emphatic- and rhetoric-driven writing. We are consciously telling our reader how we want them to read and not just giving them the words to do with what they will.

Commas have a slightly more balanced feel, giving the information equal status to everything else in the sentence. Dashes, on the other hand, are a bit more shouty, making whatever is between or after them stand out above the rest of the sentence.

So why would we choose parentheses over comma or dashes? If we have loads of either already, parentheses give us a useful third option and help us avoid confusion. If our added info is a date, or alternate spelling, it HAS to be parentheses—an em dash or comma just will not do.

Use Brackets for Clarity

These fastidious little guys ([ ]) neaten up direct quotations, clarify pronouns, and translate jargon for the rest of us mere mortals. Again, they are not vital parts of the sentence; they are nice to have.

A courtesy to nudge the reader along.

HOW TO BEAT THE SNOBS
A Bit of Guidance

Keep both parentheses and brackets out of formal writing as much as possible. Letting them romp through every other sentence makes writing hard to follow—at best. That said, a very carefully placed pair spark joy in writing. So if we want to boss around a sentence once in a while, we should know how to punctuate them.

The rules are simple. Parentheses can tame full sentences, single words, or sentence fragments without a period or opening capital letter.

If we want to add a phrase or sentence fragment mid-sentence (like this little gem), all the punctuation remains outside. No capital, no comma, no period.

Go ahead and slam down any other punctuation in parenthesis (maybe, say, we fancy showing off a bit), then we use all the commas, dashes, semicolons we want, but we still would not use a capital or period (unless we have a couple of sentences in the parenthesis. But, really, avoid that).

(If the parentheses open and close around an entire sentence, and there are no other words in the sentence, open with a capital, then stick the period before the closing parenthesis, like this.)

Exclamation points and question marks are allowed in only if they would naturally be there (understand?).

Now, brackets join the party.

If we have a regular sentence, like this one, and we want to add some quip (which is "a little witticism" not, in fact, my surname [a mistake one server made when she reserved a table for Quips]) with parentheses AND brackets, this is how we do it.

It got quite cluttered up in there, didn't it? Generally best to keep parentheses and brackets to a minimum.

> Which Wicked Witch [West or East] did Dorothy's house land on?

> They [the Munchkins] thanked them [Dorothy and friends] for seeing her [the Wicked Witch of the East] off.

Brackets are also good at throwing shade at a writer who misspelled or misused a word. Ever seen "[sic]"? It is a joy for pedant hunters. Because quotations must be presented word for word, "[sic]" (which, of course, we all know is short for **sic erat scriptum, "thus was it written"**) gives us the chance to say we know this guy is wrong, but we will let him represent himself and share his words exactly. Use it wisely, though.

> There's a lot of red smock [sic] when the Wicked Witch of the West first appears.

For the most part, though, brackets belong in math, science, and academic writing as well as in techy jargon and translation.

> The four oceans [Pacific, Atlantic, Indian, and Arctic] cover 71 percent of our planet.

> Metadata [data about other data] plays a considerable role in tracking consumer habits and preferences.

PS: AP does not even acknowledge the bracket's existence—all its jobs are covered by big-brother parenthesis, which AP is also not a huge fan of. AP would rather we just rewrite and/or keep our opinions to ourselves.

HISTORY LESSON
Parenthesis

One Richard Mulcaster of the 16th century explains parentheses best: "Parenthesis is expressed by two half circles, which in writing enclose some perfit branch, as not mere impertinent, so not fullie concident to the sentence, which it breaketh, and in reading warneth us, that the words inclosed by them ar to be pronounced with a lower & quikker voice, then the words either before them or after them."

But before those two half circles—or lunulae—appeared at the end of the 14th century, there was parenthesis. Parenthesis was (and still is) a Greek rhetoric device designed to persuade and manipulate the audience by toying with their emotions. And, in a way, it still does. Parenthesis, which we can now spot easily thanks to parenthese, takes us closer to the writer's opinions, feelings, thoughts than any other type of writing.

Think again of our dear Shakespearean actor. He knew when he should lean into the audience and deliver his line for them alone to "hear." That is what our modern parentheses do—they tell us when to come in closer and listen.

The 16th-century grammar buffs started to scatter parentheses hither and yon, especially to make metaphor and simile stand out. Down the years, though, they have fallen in and out of fashion. The Victorians were not fans, but since then they have rejoined us, having found a happy home in satire and pointed commentary.

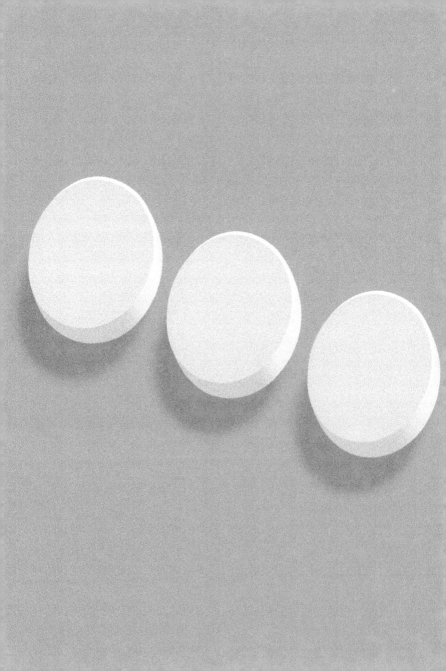

CHAPTER TWELVE
THE ELLIPSIS

What we know as ellipsis, those three dots . . . started out as more than just a punctuation mark. It used to mean taking something out. It was not until the early 20th century that it became the "dot dot dot" of Mamma Mia fame—how we format the ellipsis, we will come to later.

Like the exclamation point and em dash—the other glory-boys of punctuation—ellipsis is enjoying a renaissance. Its penchant for emotion fuels our chattiness and excitement on social media, it shares our uncertainty and concern, and it leaves a quiet space for empathy.

The Ellipsis

For the longest time, "ellipsis" just meant things were missing. Sometimes writers indicated it with dashes, spaces, or dots. But while the rhetorical ellipsis has a long history, the three-dot ellipsis only really got going in the early 20th century, with the birth of modernism.

The modernist period was a time when authors and poets turned their backs on traditional themes to toy with the stream of consciousness. They explored humanity's inner life, the silence where confusion, distress, and uncertainty linger. They poked at the intimate connections between humans and the fundamental skill we have of being able to finish each other's . . .

It was a time when writers used ellipsis to show "the sort of indefiniteness that is characteristic of all human conversations, and particularly of all English conversations, that are almost always conducted entirely by means of allusions and unfinished sentences," as author Ford Maddox Ford put it so neatly.

Modernist poet T.S. Eliot's "The Love Song of J. Alfred Prufrock," has a silent heaving sigh as his protagonist considers his end with two simple ellipses: "I grow old . . . I grow old . . ." Reading it is borderline agony, tapping a fear and a longing in all of us.

The Joyces, Eliots, Woolfs, Faulkners, and F. Scott Fitzgeralds were all at it, ellipsising here, there, and everywhere, engaging in emotions that, until then, had been hidden away, out of sight.

British super-singer Adele used the ellipsis to launch her album back in 2015, and the internet exploded. All the meaning, feeling, tension created by three little dots show the effect these rhetoric devices can have. Think of what we can do when we master them. Silence is, after all, an incredibly powerful thing . . .

The popularity of our ellipsis grew out of modernism's need in the early 20th century to express emotion and explore ideas that had been quashed in the Victorian Era. Those Victorians really were a repressed bunch, happy for morality to dominate. Ellipsis, in its own small way, helped to break that.

Now ellipses are everywhere—email, texts, Facebook, WhatsApp—they even have us on tenterhooks as someone texts back, building our anticipation for their response. They are every-where and losing power fast. We need to spend time with these three little magicians. Yes, three. Three dots. Not five. Certainly not ten. Three.

Use to Show Information Is Missing From a Sentence

Ellipsis means words or phrases have been cut from a sentence either for effect or for brevity. For brevity, we choose the bits from someone else's quote and add three dots to say, "Blah blah, blah, there's more here, but meh."

Here is Andrew Carnegie, founder of U.S. Steel Corporation and philanthropist to help.

> "Be king in your dreams. Make your vow that you will reach that position, with untarnished reputation, and make no other vow to distract your attention."

HOW TO BEAT THE SNOBS
Spacing Ellipses

Spacing with ellipses is where things get tricky because of style guides. There are just three dots to play with here, but the variety of formats is impressive, to say the least. Obviously, this works for our side when the pedants are on the prowl. "Oh, you use no space in your ellipsis—do you have a background in journalism?" we can say.

Journalists, historically, have little space to play with, so when they do use ellipsis (which is rarely), they close them up.

> **A new teenager in the house...how lucky!**

Academia, book publishing, and science as a whole like to spread out, using three periods with spaces between each one for their ellipsis. They have the space.

> **A new teenager in the house . . . how lucky!**

But in my time as a copy editor, I have seen

> A sentence here... a sentence here
>
> A sentence here ...a sentence here
>
> A sentence here ... a sentence here
>
> A sentence here. . .a sentence here

. . . and the chaotic:

> A sentence here..........a sentence here.

What the . . . ?

And with periods, remember, if we shorten a longer quotation, we go period+ellipsis (four dots).

> CMS, MLA, and APA like this: . . . .
>
> and AP prefers this: . ...

If we want reflective space, no period, just the ellipsis (three dots).

> If only we . . .

CMS and AP say no period at all. Leave the ellipsis to trail off into contemplation. MLA and APA would not touch this use of ellipsis with a ten-foot pole—far too wishy-washy.

Bored! Cut to the chase:

> **"Be king in your dreams . . . make no other vow to distract your attention."**

MLA, here, would like us to use square brackets to show the omission is not from the original quotation:

> "Be king in your dreams [. . .] make no other vow to distract your attention."

Pretty much everyone is clear that we pull apart longer quotations for our own benefit, so we do not add ellipsis at the beginning—the capital does a fine job of telling us where the quote starts.

If there is more at the end of our chosen quote nugget, but we want to leave it out, we add a period then the ellipsis, so four dots. Take John D. Rockefeller:

> "If you want to succeed you should strike out on new paths, rather than travel the worn paths of accepted success."

Remove that last bit and go with

> "To succeed you should strike out on new paths. . . ."

If we are using ellipsis for effect—think of the difference between a Rachel "Hi" and a Ross "Hi . . . "—we do not need a period. Using a period would be way too abrupt and kind of defeat the point. Just let it linger.

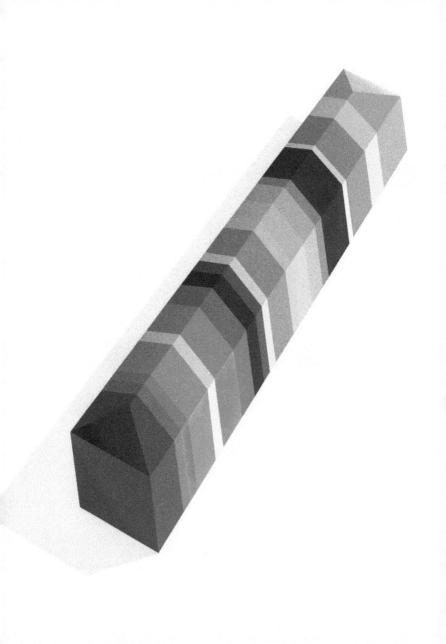

CHAPTER THIRTEEN
THE SLASH

Remember the lesson about the slash in elementary school? Remember how often that oblique little line graced papers in high school and college? No, nor do I.

Yet slash is a bit of a superstar of the punctuation world. Not a shouty, all-eyes-on-me superstar, but one of those reclusive ones who come out of normal life once or twice a year, do something impressive, then disappear again. If asked what the slash did, most of us would draw a blank. What does it do? As the forward slash, it is part of web addresses, yes. Maybe the more retro among us might have written a letter to a college friend "c/o" (care of) their parents (assuming everyone knows what a letter is). But other than that . . . ?

HISTORY LESSON
The Slash

Going back to early writing, the slash has been a big part of punctuation's journey. The slash (back then it was the virgule) appears in nearly every other punctuation point's biography; it evolved into the low dot of the period, carved a path for the comma, and behaved much like our line-continuing hyphen. It really came into its own, though, in the Middle Ages when it was the all-purpose medieval punctuation point, with Chaucer a particular fan.

But then, the master saw the protégés gain purpose of their own and leave it for dust. And there it stayed, in the dust, appearing in poetry quotations and scientific papers few people (realistically) would ever read. Even the relatively powerless en dash took slash's role of joining two words of equal weight (singer–songwriter).

Then the 1960s happened. Internet daddy Tim Berners Lee not only completely changed our lives, but he also helped rebrand the slash. No longer merely used to abbreviate (c/o) or replace (per, and/or), it now almost single-handedly guides us around the web.

Things took an intriguing turn in the '70s when slash fiction appeared. Fans of cult TV shows, movies, and books wrote same-sex romances between pop-culture characters, tagging their stories with the protagonists' names, like Kirk/Spock (listed as the birthplace of slash fiction). But slash is not stopping there. Since the end of last century, "slash" has been making waves in spoken language, too.

So what makes slash so notable? How about because literally everyone knows how to use it: When we see Y/N on a form, we all know we choose one, not both. How about it stands alongside period as the only points that have crossed from written to spoken vernacular: "Saturday mornings are for house cleaning slash catching up on Netflix." How about while we get new verbs, nouns, adjectives, and adverbs almost constantly, "slash" is the only new conjunction, replacing "and" and "or." How about even Chaucer used it as commas in his epic poems. And how about the slash's role in a whole genre of literature—slash fiction.

And you were thinking of skipping this chapter. Think again.

Use with Numbers

We should start where, traditionally, slashes have their main home. In math and science. When measurements, dates, fractions, and periods of time come to play, slashes are pretty useful.

What is easier: The density of gold is 19.3 grams per cubic centimeter or 19.3 g/cm^3 In this case, 19.3 is not too onerous a number, but when we get into really big numbers—universe numbers—writing out measurements could take all day. Abbreviation here is handy. In measurements, slash takes the place of "per," and it does in most scientific writing. But the rest of us use it this way, too. Think per mile (/m), per kilometer (/km), miles per hour (m/h), calories per person per day (kcal/person/day).

Slash also hands us a consecutive period of time: The birth years of my children, 2006/07 were life changing.

And talking of dates, most of us use the slash to write the date in shorthand month/day/year, either when we are form filling or

HOW TO BEAT THE SNOBS
Talking Slash

Punctuation snobs famously dislike change. Remember that serial-comma furor? I rest my case. Yet we are seeing the most exciting change in punctuation for a while.

Since the end of last century, slash has taken its place alongside period as the only other spoken punctuation mark, leapfrogging from borderline obscurity to popular use. It is now a punctuation point of the people, for the people.

Slash's new purpose seems to be the love child of multitasking and so many of our interactions being in written form. There is a sense of furthering conversation, of offering up a choice, showing balance or maybe intention:

> I hear what you're saying **slash** hear what I'm saying.
>
> That's an idea **slash** here's a way we could make that better **slash** worse **slash** take it to another place."

Phrases around this house include

> What are you doing **slash** could you please unload the dishwasher?
>
> I've been sitting all day **slash** anyone want to take a walk?
>
> I don't want to do the dishwasher. **Slash** let's take a walk.
>
> Going to get this finished NOW. **Slash** it'll definitely be done by tomorrow morning. **Slash** afternoon.

In the great scheme of things, it is still early days for slash's new role. Will it move away from the full word (a conjunction) and back to a typographical point? Will the / step in with the same meaning or will new meaning attach to it? Given punctuation has ebbed and flowed over hundreds of years, this is definitely one to watch—and a great way to wind up a pedant. Enjoy!

just being lazy in letter writing (it is still better to write the date out in full). For fractions fans, this will be a pleasant memory. For the rest, sorry. The slash, as we all remember, is the line between the numerator (at the top) and the denominator (below), so ½, 2/3 and ¾—both versions are perfectly acceptable. Remember, though, when writing formally, fractions should be in words: one-half, two-fifths.

Use to Convey "and" or "or"

Once found lurking in legal documents, the and/or slash is even vilified in lawyers' friend *The Blue Book*, which relegates the slash to note taking, allowed nowhere near a final draft. Where we see the and/or slash most is on forms, where we all know Y/N allows us no discussion. Yes or no. Answer the question. Because, really, what better use for this wonderful old punctuation point than to replace those tiresomely long words "and" and "or"?

But and/or allows a genuine sense of balance in some cases—it embraces that middle ground, those gray areas. Like the en dash, the slash replaces "and/or" to give equal weight in a relationship or conflict. When we see a slash between vocations/jobs/roles, we know each is equally important. Ask a "singer/songwriter" or "mom/taxi/chef/maid/PA" which one they are, and prep for a loooooooong answer. We will not discuss pro-life/pro-choice, here, either.

Apply for a copywriting job, and we need "a bachelor's degree in English and/or five years' similar experience." With one or the other, we will likely be in with a shot. But the and/or slash also gives options, again equally weighted. A text I had recently asked me to make a choice: "Lasagna/burgers for dinner?" "Either/or," I helpfully replied.

Most style guides say keep the slash out of formal writing—no more sir/madam, please—but there is no question it does have a place in informal writing and note taking and, increasingly, in speech.

CHAPTER FOURTEEN
UNUSUAL CHARACTERS

With punctuation being as old as the hills, it is no surprise we have added and lost some marks along the way, and that other languages have variations on the theme.

In German and French, for example, big numbers use the comma and period, but flipped. So the period (.) is the thousand separator (English's 1,000 turns into 1.000) and the comma (,) shows the decimal place (making $10.30 $10,30). In Spanish, question marks and exclamation points turn upside-down and shift to the front of the question or exclamation, too: **¿Cuántos años tienes?** (How old are you?) We even see Western punctuation in countries with different alphabets, in Korean and Japanese, Chinese and Russian—where they pretty much do the same jobs as they do in English.

English punctuation has been as it is now since around the turn of the 20th century, with slight tweaks, here and there. Some publishing houses use more punctuation, some less, but the rules and points are fundamentally the same.

Around the mid-20th century, though, a flurry of innovative punctuation marks appeared, around the time advertising realized emotion was a nifty thing to tap into. Martin K. Speckter's interrobang is hanging on as ?!, but very few people use the actual glyph (‽). Hervé Bazin offered up six new points that never really took off. And since 2010, Paul and Douglas J. Sak have been making a valiant attempt to integrate their patented SarcMark® in digital communication, releasing apps, plug-ins, and software to launch it out into the world.

Enjoy these little gems of punctuation and feel free to share your knowledge with any snob squaring up to do grammar battle.

Use the Backward Question Mark for Rhetoric Questions and Irony

English printer Henry Denham presented the percontation point (⸮) in 1580. Its single purpose was to mark a rhetorical question, and, while it flapped along the runway for a few years, it died about 50 years after it appeared. It was a nice idea, sure, but the other printers were not fans. Scribes and writers were happy enough to use it, but what was the point if the printers would not cast new type?

What seemed to be the shoulder shrug of the punctuation world, the percontation point laid down to sleep. When it woke, nearly three hundred years later, it said, "From now on, I want people to know me for my work in irony." And so it was.

With the blessing of French poet Alcanter de Brahm and leading Belgian inventor and journalist Marcellin Jobard, the percontation point turned its back on rhetorical questions, preferring the jaunty fun of irony. In its new guise and with a new name—irony point—it was slightly smaller than its old self and rose above the line. And there it has stayed. It got very little use in the great scheme of things, but in this digital age, things are changing again.

We can now create the irony mark ⸮ using **UnicodeAlt+2e2e** (no, not by turning the keyboard upside down), and there is a groundswell of people—especially in social media world—gunning for its popular return. Go on, give it a try.

Use Bazin's Six Punctuating Inventions

In 1966, another Frenchman, one Hervé Bazin, also tried his hand at creating an irony point—ignoring the fact there was a perfectly acceptable one already available—as part of an embarrassment of new punctuation marks he dreamed up.

In his book *Plumons l'Oiseau* (*Let's Pluck the Bird*), he proposed **the acclamation point, the love point, the certitude point, the doubt point, the authority point,** and **the irony point.**

I'm delighted you could make it [∨ acclamation point]

You truly are the best [♡ love point]

Actually, the comma goes here [† certitude point]

I thought the comma went here [⸮ doubt point]

I know my stuff [⸙ authority point]

Well, aren't we impressive [ψ irony point]

It is fair to say he had a point (well, he had six, really). If we allow emotion in with question marks and exclamations, ellipses and em dashes, why should we not share our love, certainty, authority, acclaim, and doubt with punctuation points? But, much like with the backward question mark, printers were having none of it, and Bazin's inventions merely wiggled to the edge of the nest, flapped their wings, then, well . . .

They are perhaps most famous for their convincing failure to become anything more than an idea. Maybe, as is so often the case, their timing was just poor. After all, the internet was only a couple of years away—they never really stood a chance. There are still folks trying to standardize Bazin's points and put them alongside their punctuation point siblings, but at present, their efforts are in vain.

Use the Interrobang to Show Surprise or Shock

In 1962, real-life mad man Martin K. Speckter had a little more success by bundling together the question and exclamation marks, creating the most famous new symbol: **‽, the interrobang.** Speckter's "eureka!" moment was over dinner as he wondered whether Christopher Columbus was excited or doubtful when he first saw land. Would he have said, "Land, ho!" or "Land, ho?" Speckter wanted a way to show this kind of ambiguity, and, for him, ‽ was it. What a day it was‽ (both for Columbus and Speckter).

Like its ancestors, the interrobang is an evolution of existing punctuation. Think of the natural movement from Aristophanes' dots to the period, from the slash to the comma; surely interrobang was the obvious step in Speckter's advertising world?

Typed by hitting **? backspace !**, interrobang found a natural place in 1960s typewritten copy, and things seemed good to go. But printers could not print it, so the little hybrid point looked like it was on its way out. Until along came the internet, and, boy, do we love sharing our opinions, thoughts, and comments on there. Interrobang is now clinging on as **?!** and it might still be in with a chance. For a start, the symbol is in Word and is easily added to phones, and when that is too much of a struggle, a **?!** is perfectly acceptable.

Give it some love.

Use the SarcMark for Sarcasm

Oh, we love sarcasm. This verbal form of irony, though, is not always easy to spot; especially now that so much of our communication is written. It is way too easy to screw up by assuming the person we are writing to will clearly know we are being sarcastic. And they do not.

The brainchild of Doug and Paul Sak, **the SarcMarc** (short for "sarcasm mark") debuted in 2010. The copyrighted, patented, and trademarked point had big plans to help the world embrace sarcasm—at a price (literally, we have to buy it).

Given there is a similar mark called **the snark mark (.~)**, which is copyright free and free free, history alone can us tell how successful the SarcMark will be.

In using either the snark mark or SarcMark, we are telling our reader to dig a little deeper into the meaning, that not all is as it seems on first glance. That we have our snarky, sarcastic hat on.

Great surprise party.~ Good job Dad didn't give the game away.

Use Hashtags for Self-Reflection, Irony, and Public Comment

Grab a hashtag, throw together an unpunctuated phrase and, boom, we have what looks like something Aristophanes tried very hard to put an end to more than two thousand years ago. He would be turning in his tomb.

Wander through the Twittersphere or Instaworld and we quickly stumble across #parentingfail #facepalm #mysuperpower alongside the everyday #throwbackthursday, #lifegoals, #love, #photooftheday #motivation. Hashtag, hashtag, hashtag.

The hashtag used to be called **an octothorp** as well as **the pound sign** and **the number sign**. Its main function in recent history was to highlight something in coding (not going into that any further!).

But now. Oh, now. It helps us provide a running commentary to EV.ERY.THING in our informal, digital writing. Hashtags let us go on tangents, make snarky comments about ourselves and everyone else, about life. We can be #jokingnotjoking, we can #imeanit, we can have #noclue.

Hashtags share our allegiances, our beliefs, and help us join the bigger conversation. Think #metoo. They build context, they extend an idea, they dive deeper without having to say too much more. And that is just on the face of it—that is just the part we see.

In the background, they organize, target audiences, increase brand engagement, filter content, tell the world what is trending, guide us to our kindred spirits wherever they are on the planet.

And we thought we had a long to-do list.

Use Emojis and Gifs for Everything

Emote icon. Emoticon. Emojis. Now gifs. What next?!

I was drawing smiley faces on pen-letters back in the '80s, and it would be fair to bet people drew faces in their communications for a very long time before that, too. They have definitely taken on a life of their own in the last few years, however. Movies, merch, more inclusive emoji, bigger gif libraries. It is perfectly possible now to have an entire conversation with emoji and gifs and never have to type an actual word. But does that mean emoji and gifs are a new form of communication in themselves or are they just helping words out? Do they need punctuation or are they punctuation?

For the most part, emoji still have a punctuating role, sharing space with or after full sentences, adding emotion (go figure) and color to the words we write. Generally speaking, emoji and gifs tend to take their place at the end of a sentence or immediately after we have sent a worded message to add comment, meaning, when we feel the words might not have been enough.

It should go without saying that emoji and gifs are playful and should never step across into formal writing, but I doubt that is why the style guides have little to say about them. The debate has not really started about whether either of these could be considered punctuation—and they might not be around long enough to warrant that conversation. Who knows?!

CHAPTER FIFTEEN
THE "NOT PUNCTUATION POINTS"

True story. Some people think @, &, and all those dots and lines found above words in other languages are punctuation points. But they are not.

Nor, fun fact, is the "Morgan Freemark" (created by CollegeHumor to nudge readers to use Morgan Freeman's resonant voice when reading). Who knew?

While it might be tough to mistake the Morgan Freemark for a punctuation point, it makes sense that people might confuse the ampersand (&), registration mark (®), number sign (#), and so on for legit punctuation points. They are not letters, on the face of it. They appear in sentences. But do they add meaning, nuance, or sense to a sentence? Not really. And that is why they are not punctuation points.

The purpose of punctuation is to help us organize our writing, so readers can get from beginning to end in the way we want them to. We can add stress, pauses, and sense with punctuation.

The @ and & guys are characters or typographical marks, kind of like shorthand. They give us quick way of writing a word (because, let's face it, "at" and "and" take a long old time to write in full). And the accents, lines, and squiggles above and below letters are called diacritic symbols. In many languages, they tell the reader how to pronounce a word; we know, for example, to use the hard c for "cat," but some languages would add a little diacritic mark to make it clear it is "kat" not "sat."

Meet & (Ampersand)

Shock, horror: & was once the 27th member of the alphabet. Right there after Z.

Children reciting the alphabet (& included) would have to say "per se" when a letter was also a word by itself (because that is what per se means, "by itself"—not "as such" as some people seem to think). Thus, the song would go "A, per se A, B, C, D, E, F, G, H, I per se I, J, K, LMNOP . . . W, X, Y, Z, & per se and." Granted, it does not have quite the same rhythm to it.

Those kids would belt out "& per se and," but just as we hurtled through grace at my secondary school, "Forwhatweareabouttore-ceivemaytheLordmakeustrulythankfulamen," the kids wanted to move on to the next thing, ASAP. So "& per se and" became "ampersand." See, children really can make a difference.

The & symbol started life as the Latin et, which means "and." Old-time scribes loved their flourishy writing, and over time, the two letters merged/blended to become the & we use today.

And how do we use it today? Most publishing houses prefer to avoid & in running copy and headlines, but it has found a place in business names, advertising, commercial signs, where space is tight on websites, and in abbreviations like B&B, R&D, R&R.

> **I'm looking forward to some R&R in the B&B after an intense session of R&D.**

Some house styles are happy to use & in titles. It is a matter of taste. All power to the people who love an ampersand. Best to avoid it, though.

Meet @

Like the ampersand, @ takes the place of longer words. Yes, it means "at" in modern use, but journey a little way back, and it stood in for thousands of uses of "at," "toward," "by," and "about" in Biblical manuscripts. It has also represented weights and measures, essentially "so many things for this price," from wine to wheat to apples from the convenience store.

@ goes way back—even further than the dawn of email in the '70s. It is 1345, and the people's one desire is a Bulgarian translation of a Constantinos Manasses chronicle. And down there at the "Amen" an @ stands where the capital A was: @men. Literally no one knows why, including the Vatican Apostolic Library, where it now calls home.

Fast-forward to 1971 . . . where one Ray Tomlinson, a pioneering computer programmer, has managed to send messages to different users on one computer, but he wants to send a message to someone on another machine. He needs to split the recipient's name and digital address; he spots the @ sign on the keyboard. Thus the email address was born. A slice of history: The first email ever sent went to tomlinson@bbn.tenexa to the machine sitting next to him.

And still that is @'s main job. Good luck sending an email without it. In the social media world, @ helps us name or get the attention of a person in our public posts. But in any long-form writing, beyond bookkeeping, it has no place.

A bit of fun to astound those pedants with, though, are the names it has in other languages: Swiss say "monkey's tail"; Greeks use "duckling"; in Hungarian, it is "worm"; Kazakh, "dog's head"; Serbian, "crazy A"; Bulgarian, "little monkey"; and Taiwanese, "little mouse."

How to Use Diacritic Marks

Diacritic marks are also not punctuation points, even if they feel like they might be. Diacritic marks are the lines, accents, dots, wiggles in other languages, and they change the way a letter sounds in a word. English has no diacritic marks of its own. Instead, we stole the words with diacritic marks (née, façade, naïve, über) and, in a bout of jealousy, stripped them of their diacritics and claimed them as our own.

English is such a rich language, created in the twists and turns of history, influenced by invaders and colonists, immigrants and regional dialects. Over the centuries, we have tucked all manner of words from other languages into our dictionaries to wave around as our own. Many of those words came with diacritic marks in the beginning, but, in English, they have not stayed the course. Naïve is now naive, façade is facade, and cliché is cliche. Sad but true.

Many style houses tell us to drop diacritic marks if the word is so integrated into English that it is in the dictionary: doppelganger, resume, pate (this poor thing has lost two diacritic marks; in its original French, it was pâté). If you do see a pedant trucking out a diacritic, you know what, let it go—it might be a nice conversation starter, and you can absolutely hold your own with diacritics.

How to Use the Morgan Freemark

What a way to end a book about punctuation: citing a made-up, non-punctuation point that encourages the reader to assume the voice of the acting legend, Morgan Freeman.

Dovetailing the phrase we want spoken in Morgan Freeman's voice are Morgan Freeman–style quotation marks. The wry smile of the great actor peers out at us and we just know we want those deep, smooth, knowing tones to pep up our phrase.

Who knows? It might even catch on.

Style Guides

Punctuation has some hard-and-fast rules, but there are some rules that are only hard and fast depending on who dictates our style.

If we are writing a novel or nonfiction book, our house style will be a version of *Chicago Manual of Style* (which is what this book follows, for the most part). If the law is our thing, we will turn to *The Blue Book*. For academic publications, the Modern Language Association forms the basis of most academic journals' styles. American Psychological Association, on the other hand, is at the heart of writing for engineering, social sciences, and business.

While mainly following these styles, each journal, paper, magazine, website, whatever will push boundaries, add nuance, and explore alternates to create a unique style sheet (probably just to keep copy editors on our toes!).

The following quick reference tables cover the majority of the elements that differ from guide to guide.

CONTINUED ▶

Punctuation Mark	CHICAGO MANUAL OF STYLE (CMS)	AMERICAN PSYCHOLOGICAL ASSOCIATION (APA)	MODERN LANGUAGE ASSOCIATION (MLA)	THE BLUE BOOK	ASSOCIATED PRESS (AP)
	Book publishing	Engineering, social sciences, and business	Academic journals and research	Legal documents	Newsprint
Serial comma	Yes	Yes	Yes	Yes	No
Introductory comma	Yes	Yes	Yes	Yes	No
Spaces after period	1	2	1	1	1
Caps after colon	two+ sentences = cap	One independent clause = cap	Use lowercase when the word that follows the colon is normally lower case. Use a capital letter when the colon introduces a rule, principle, or several related clauses	Writer's choice for one independent clause two+ sentences = cap	One independent clause = cap
Possessive/ -s ending plurals (**boss'** or **boss's**)	s's	s's	s's	s's	s'
Primary quotation marks	" "	" "	" "	" "	" "
Secondary quotation marks (within a quotation)	' '	' '	' '	' '	' '

Punctuation Mark	CHICAGO MANUAL OF STYLE (CMS)	AMERICAN PSYCHOLOGICAL ASSOCIATION (APA)	MODERN LANGUAGE ASSOCIATION (MLA)	THE BLUE BOOK	ASSOCIATED PRESS (AP)
Punctuation Mark	Book publishing	Engineering, social sciences, and business	Academic journals and research	Legal documents	Newsprint
Post-noun dictionary-listed hyphen	no compound hyphen after the noun	dictionary compound hyphens retained after the noun e.g. **she was good-looking, steak was well-done**	dictionary compound hyphens retained after the noun e.g. **she was good-looking, steak was well-done**	dictionary compound hyphens retained after the noun e.g. **she was good-looking, steak was well-done**	dictionary compound hyphens retained after the noun e.g. **she was good-looking, steak was well-done**
Post-noun hyphenation	only hyphenate for clarity	never hyphenate post noun	never hyphenate post noun	only hyphenate for clarity	Only hyphenate post noun following a form of "to be"
Hyphen in fractions as nouns	hyphenate fractions: **two-thirds, one-quarter**	Do not hyphenate fractions: **two thirds, one quarter**			
Hyphens in shared nationalities	African American				African-American
Prefix		hyphenate before a capital (**pre-WW2**) or a number (**post-2000**) and to prevent confusion (**re-cover/recover** or **antiaircraft**)			
Em dash spacing	**word—word**	word—word	word—word	word—word	one either side of each em dash: **word — word**

CONTINUED ▶

Punctuation Mark	CHICAGO MANUAL OF STYLE (CMS)	AMERICAN PSYCHOLOGICAL ASSOCIATION (APA)	MODERN LANGUAGE ASSOCIATION (MLA)	THE BLUE BOOK	ASSOCIATED PRESS (AP)
	Book publishing	Engineering, social sciences, and business	Academic journals and research	Legal documents	Newsprint
Slash	Do not use	Do not use	Do not use	Acceptable	Do not use
Ellipsis with period	. . . .	. . . .	. . . .	. . . .	. . . .

Index

Acknowledgments

The first thank you goes to Steve, my real husband and office husband, for sharing office space despite my very loud, excitable typing; for picking up the slack when commas and semicolons have distracted me; and for listening to my endless lists. This book is NOW finished. Officially.

Thank you also to my fabulous children, who have done a great job of feigning interest when I wax lyrical about ellipsis, commas, and the weirder histories of punctuation. Thank you, too, to my parents, the greatest supporters and best sounding boards a daughter could ask for. And to my grandma for just being. I love you all very much.

And to Susy, who encouraged me every step of the way and made me believe I could do it. Even the hard bits.

About the Author

Lucy Cripps is an incorrigible pedant—for your sanity don't get her started on serial commas or the abuse of exclamation marks. It's a lesson her writing clients—Red Bull, Engadget, Expedia, Clarks—have learned. As have the students on the Business Writing courses she teaches for the Professional Writing Academy, the UK's leading online writing school.

Where did this infatuation with language come from? She can nail it down to the terrifying moment she stood in front of final-year undergrads at Salzburg University, Austria, to teach the Advanced Writing Skills course. And the students knew more than she did.

In that instant, she decided she wanted to be someone who "knows her stuff." Around the same time, she embarked on an MA in Professional Writing, and driven by her new motto, worked night and day to stay ahead of the students and write a book about punctuation and grammar.

Her passion grew in her five years at Salzburg, teaching grammar, writing and editing courses—all with a focus on US grammar and punctuation. There was nothing more satisfying than when her friend with a linguistics PhD said: "Wow, you know your stuff. If ever I have a punctuation question, you're always the one I come to."

Lucy is now a full-time freelance wordsmith living in Bristol, UK, and ghostauthor with journalist Daoud Kuttab of the memoir, *Sesame Street, Palestine.*

Words, editing, and language are Lucy's biggest hobbies—so, technically, she hasn't done a day's work in her life. When not writing, editing, or being Mom, Lucy rows and snowboards.